Fall and Winter Turkey Hunter's Handbook

Steve Hickoff

STACKPOLE BOOKS

D0913704

Published by

STACKPOLE BOOKS
5067 Ritter Road
Mechanicsburg, PA 17055
www.stackpolebooks.com

Printed in China

First edition

10 9 8 7 6 5 4 3 2 1

Cover design by Wendy A. Reynolds
Cover photograph by John Hafner
Photographs by author, except where otherwise noted

Library of Congress Cataloging-in-Publication Data

Hickoff, Steve, 1958-
  Fall and winter turkey hunter's handbook / Steve Hickoff. — 1st ed.
      p. cm.
  Includes bibliographical references and index.
  ISBN-10: 0-8117-3406-4
  ISBN-13: 978-0-8117-3406-6
  1. Turkey hunting. I. Title.

SK325.T8H53 2007
799.2'4645—dc22

2006037888

To Midge March Madness, my flock-flushing English setter: sweet-hearted upland renegade, companion in the autumn turkey woods, and bunkmate on the road. It would have been so much less without her.

CONTENTS

FOREWORD

In the spring of '05, my wife Julie and I killed the Grand Slam as a couple. We did four states, including Iowa twice, tagged an even dozen longbeards, and piled up hours upon hours of missed sack time. From March 8 to May 16, I lost 17 pounds. . . . Sleep deprivation, an unholy amount of walking, and meals consisting solely of Atomic Fire Balls, Gatorade, and generic cereal bars—that's the life-sustaining part!—will do that to a body.

And I loved every minute of it. In fact, there were times when I had no tag, and I couldn't convince anyone, even strangers, to be my gunman. So I went out, gunless and tagless, just to listen. Just to hear that gobble one more time. Let me tell you, it was absolutely awesome.

Now, I'm not telling you this to brag. Honestly, I'm not. I'm saying it all simply . . . well, simply to say that I've got this thing about turkeys. About turkey hunting. About being there, right in the middle of it, when that old gobbler breaks his nightlong silence and announces to the world that he, without question, is the boss of everything around him. Yes, sir. Just writing it puts a knot in my throat and starts me thinking that I'm moving around too much.

That's spring. But there's another turkey time, for lack of a better phrase, that doesn't get near the attention or the recognition it should. That's fall, and while I'm a huge fan of busting flocks of hens with their long-legged, tag-along jakes and jennies—you see, folks, I like eating 'em as much as I like hunting 'em—the months of September, October, and into winter . . . well, that's Steve Hickoff's time of year.

Hickoff's a brother in arms, a journalistic misfit from whom, I think, I was separated at birth. A twin-sons-of-different-mothers sort of thing, and I certainly do send my apologies to Misters Fogelberg and Weisberg for borrowing their line. But song lyrics aren't the point here; the point here is Steve Hickoff and turkeys.

Once a month during the fall, the phone will ring. "We had a great hunt in Vermont," the voice will say. "Midge did a fine job. Found two flocks; busted 'em both. Buddy killed one on the call-back, and then we did it again." It's Hickoff, and he's talking like an eight-year-old who knows damn well that he's going to the playground and not to the dentist. He's on a roll; I (surprisingly enough, just ask my wife) don't interrupt. This is all too good. Eventually he slows, but not until I've lived each break and each bird and every opportunity, filled or missed. It's refreshing in this age of "Hey, what did he score?" whitetails, that to Steve, the kill doesn't matter. In fact, the fall of the hammer is actually anticlimactic, for the man would rather spend more time describing Midge's performance or the turkeys she flushed or the painter's palette that is the autumn countryside and—Heaven help me for saying this—the one that got away. I like that about him . . . but I like the fact, too, that he likes to eat 'em as much as I do.

This isn't Steve's first full-length work, but it's his finest. Why? Because the information and the stories contained within all come straight from the field. The result of hardcore, firsthand experience presented by a guy who lives these very words on a daily basis each and every fall. But more important, this material—and I feel almost ashamed for trivializing it so—comes straight from the heart. All handed to you, dear reader, by a man with a passion for the sights and the colors and the sounds—and let's not forget the dogs!—that make fall turkey hunting the incredible outdoor experience it is.

So come on along—it's going to be one hell of a ride. I can guarantee that. I just hope I can get some sleep along the way, and that Hickoff brought something other than those damn cereal bars.

—M. D. Johnson

PREFACE

Thanksgiving falls in November for a reason.
Unlike any previous title, this book will provide the
modern wild turkey enthusiast with a user's guide for scouting,
hunting, and thinking about this great American gamebird in
autumn and winter. Most modern turkey hunting books only
emphasize the spring season—an annual activity I also enjoy on
hunts around the country. If fall and winter turkey hunting is mentioned at all, the coverage is cursory at best, and at times, almost
apologetic. My effort here will complement such existing works by
adding a comprehensive second-season perspective dealing with
the unique autumn through winter phase of our tradition.

Antlered game dominates the attention of many between Labor Day
and the Christmas holiday, then into the New Year. The outdoor industry
reflects this in their advertising and marketing push. Antlers rule. This
focus is reflected in many publications where my work appears. Praise
the editor who lets this fall and winter turkey writer have his say in those
places, wedged between the whitetail, elk, and moose narratives, and for
those who assign fall and winter pieces for the turkey magazines. I don't
fault anyone for having a different quarry in mind once the maple leaves
blush red and flurries fall. Like other turkey addicts, though, I can't help
myself, and desire no remedy other than more time in the woods with the
birds. It's my hope that both veterans and newcomers alike will read this
work, and finally see why some of us are year-round turkey hunters.

This turkey book is a collection of philosophical hunting how-to,
where-to, and why-to. In the chapters that follow, I'll try to characterize
the pursuit's traditional roots, the joys of pre-season scouting, and the
necessity of securing permission to hunt. Hunters speak the language of

these big birds. As a result, material here will also discuss the fall and winter turkey's vocabulary, how to listen better to hear these birds, and how to replicate those calls with manmade devices. Locating fall and winter roosts, identifying changing flock composition, and hunting fall and winter gobblers are detailed here, plus my reflections on the turkey dogging tradition, a practice I enjoy each autumn. You'll find plenty of strategies earned over decades of hunting, including sidebars of additional information within individual sections. Additionally, some of the material on firearms, ammunition, and archery tackle will benefit all turkey hunters, fall, winter, or spring. Some thoughts on shooting, safety, hunting where-to, and the future of our enthusiasm conclude this book, along with an appendix of recommended reading and product-related contact information.

Think of it as my own lengthy monologue on the fall and winter turkey woods. It's up to you, finally, to experience your own personal story. Get out there whenever you can.

ACKNOWLEDGMENTS

Wild turkey enthusiasts are members of an extended family, and I'm glad to have met every one of you. Turkey hunters—who also happen to edit national magazines and assign articles on the subject—deserve appreciative mention. There have been many, including Gene Smith, Brian Lovett, Gerry Bethge, Doug Howlett, and Jim Schlender to name a handful. Thanks go out to all of them, including the good folks at Stackpole Books, especially Judith Schnell and Don Gulbrandsen, who took initial interest in this project, then sustained it. Keep in touch. I like the work.

M. D. Johnson, who wrote the foreword, Jim Casada, who provided the encomium, and John Hafner, for his photographic contributions, all have my gratitude. John and J. T. Byrne, Ernie Calandrelli, Pete and Sherry Clare, Dodd Clifton, Ray Eye, and Gary Sefton have shared memorable hunts over the years. After decades of writing, the entire list of outdoor-industry professionals to whom I'm indebted reads like a Pro-Bowl roster.

The National Wild Turkey Federation (NWTF) also deserves mention for its ongoing pro-hunting conservation endeavor, and educational projects regarding this great gamebird. If you aren't a member, consider it. Rob Keck, and others at this organization, have my appreciation.

This hunting fraternity also includes good friends and acquaintances afflicted with a passion for this gamebird. Thanks especially to turkey buds Marc Brown, Paul Carlton, and Lawrence Pyne, and to the many turkey hunters and landholders who share their property: folks like John and Donna Parker in Kentucky, members of the Unionville Sportsman's Club in Missouri, Kevin Evans, and Rodney Brazie in New York State.

None of this would be possible without my family, of course. My father, who first took me turkey hunting in the early 1970s, provided the early example. Later my brothers Dave and Ron shared hunts as well, while our mother encouraged us to cook everything we brought home. All the gun dogs I've ever gone afield with arouse deep and thoughtful reflections every day. Outside of spring turkey hunting when I go it alone, they make autumn and winter upland days better for me.

Finally, my loving wife and daughter give me free rein to turkey hunt around the country, far more than any husband or daddy should be permitted. To Elizabeth and Cora, all my love. My better half once left a note after my pre-dawn departure hours before, a scribbled countertop message that read: "Good morning—I didn't even hear you get up (or hear the coffee maker). If you got a turkey, call me. If you didn't get a turkey, call me, and then nap. If you got a buck, call Fish & Game and turn yourself in."

I still haven't bothered much with the deer, not even in the off-season. Turkeys are just too damn appealing.

The Thanksgiving Bird

At least superficially, the American wild turkey needs no introduction. Still, at times, this upland bird remains a pleasant mystery.

While the uninitiated might ask if your wild Thanksgiving table fare tastes gamy—preferring store-bought farm birds with handy pop-up timers—and though some children's book illustrators might depict strutting adult gobblers without beards, non-hunters can at least identify what they're seeing—even at 65 mph as they pass a dark wad of big birds on farmland.

This handbook is for the person who feels the leaf-whispering pull of the painted October woods. It's for the veteran autumn enthusiast who seeks to fuel annual off-season anticipation before the hunt begins. It's for the sportsman who thrills at the booming gobble of a spring tom during the mating season, but who wants to extend that exhilarating feeling. Fall and winter turkey hunts sustain in many ways.

For some, the freewheeling spring gobbler phase may have meant hunting early on in March, as I have in states like Florida and Alabama. After this, April may have included visiting Texas for Rio Grande turkeys, or a Midwestern state or two, such as Iowa or Missouri where some of my biggest longbeards have been tagged, or out West where Merriam's turkeys roost. In the Northeast, hunting continues well into May, tags providing. I've taken a New England gobbler as late as Memorial Day. Maine's recent spring season didn't close until the first week of June, long after folks down in Lone Star State hill country sought shade after their hunts ended.

Then it's over, abruptly. Withdrawal symptoms kick in big-time, despite the fact you are sleeping regularly now, and speaking human language more often than wild turkey—or at least trying to.

That's when my thoughts immediately turn toward fall, with a steady interest in watching for those first flocks to appear in the form of a brood hen leading her charges along in grassy areas where they bug for protein-rich insects. Those who have never heard the word "bug" used as a verb should know that this activity is sustained for months on end, as fuzzy poults grow into juvenile birds the size of the brood hen. Autumn is coming, and they instinctively know it as the days shorten. You do too.

As turkey season arrives—sometimes first as an archery-only option, technically in late summer—those who have watched flocks throughout the barbecue months now feel the pull of game time. You want to be out there where the action is.

As mentioned, some states only permit archery tackle, where you'll experience the true meaning of catch and release (turkeys called into range, and missed with the stick and string), as I have during New Hampshire's autumn bow season, which starts in September and ends in December. Ironically, failing to close the deal on a legal bird prolongs the enjoyment. Firearm seasons arrive elsewhere soon enough, often in October, when you'll decide either to fill a tag on a bird-of-the-year—called into range after a flock break—or whether to up the stakes and hold out for a mature longbeard.

Despite what you've read elsewhere, you'll hear fall birds gobble, and even see some strut as they sort out the morning's pecking order. You'll marvel at the vast array of calls autumn wild turkeys can make, because at no other time will you hear such a range of wonderful racket in the woods, from birds-of-the-year to adult hens and gobblers. You may pattern flocks as an archer does deer, and set up to score. You may utilize a dog to find and flush flocks in states like Virginia or New York where it's legal, and then conceal that canine companion in the blind as you call scattered turkeys back into shotgun range. You may even use a rifle while ghosting along in places like Pennsylvania's hardwood ridge tops, where I first turkey hunted as a teenager in the early 1970s.

As the first snowflakes begin to fall, you'll savor the declining daylight, enjoy your woodstove fires, and recall autumn turkey hunts more than once to patient, tolerant spouses. You'll want to hold on to the fine memories, and if blessed by your efforts, you'll celebrate Thanksgiving dinner with a wild bird on the table. Gamy tasting? Not at all. Wild turkey is delicious. Chances are you'll even hunt turkeys after this annual holiday, as seasons run into the New Year. Fine meals extend your hunting.

No matter how long you hunt this grand quarry, you keep coming back for more: scouting, watching, hunting, talking about, and celebrating the bird on your holiday supper table. Fall and winter turkey hunting has a rich historical tradition.

CHAPTER 1

Wild flocks thrive due to sound management efforts, providing opportunities in the turkey woods fall, winter, and spring.

JOHN HAFNER PHOTO

The Tradition,
Then and Now

At first there were no rules, and now there are many. Modern hunting seasons rightly insist on fair chase, where the quarry has a better chance of winning than you do. Regulated spring, fall, and winter seasons ensure the steady growth and stability of turkey populations. Resource conservation demands it in the face of habitat loss and shifting cultural viewpoints. Thanks to attentive management and the bird's marvelous adaptability, wild flocks thrive. The classic age of American wild turkey hunting is now.

In recent history, management regulations have provided the basis for hunters to pursue their chosen quarry, with expanding options as flock numbers grow. While some might choose to only chase spring gobblers, opting to target antlered game in the fall, serious turkey enthusiasts—and even those who casually dabble with it—find autumn and winter hunting uniquely challenging.

When Europeans first arrived in North America, they encountered abundant wild turkey flocks, and as a result market hunting flourished—for a while, that is. Unfortunately this unregulated pursuit yielded diminished returns, as wild turkey populations inevitably dwindled. Habitat from the East to Midwest was plowed and cleared. Many areas no longer sustained flocks. Over-harvesting this resource would later teach the modern wildlife manager a lesson, albeit delayed. Effective management strategies wouldn't emerge until well into the twentieth century. Even then such efforts ranged from ineffective and experimental (stocked game-farm birds) to substantially viable (the trap-and-transfer of wild turkeys later released into appropriate habitats).

Modern sensibilities have changed profoundly since John James Audubon (1785–1851) wrote on the subject. An avid hunter, naturalist, and painter of birds—though his version of the turkey gobbler is mysteriously sub-par—his travel writing depicted the early nineteenth-century North American range succumbing to development pressure. A brief glimpse into his journals illustrates the frequent taking of any wild thing, including turkeys, on an unregulated, as-desired basis, either baited by grain or by other surefire methods.

It's clear that resources were perceived as unlimited. Any strategy of securing wild turkeys was acceptable, the notion of fair chase had yet to evolve, and market hunting absorbed the numbers. Wildlife management had yet to assert a sense of scientific principles, game laws were liberal at best, and restoration efforts were far off. Times change. Out of this relentless pursuit of North American turkey flocks emerged seasons, limits, law enforcement, and appropriate sporting tactics for taking this grand gamebird.

Other writers reflected this change, too. During the twentieth century, classics such as Edward A. McIlhenny's 1914 work *The Wild Turkey and Its Hunting* (writing composed initially by Charles L. Jordan, who met with an untimely death before its publication—shot by a poacher in 1909), and Henry E. Davis's *The American Wild Turkey* (1949) characterized the emergent tactics and hunting strategies based on respect for the quarry and evolving sportsmanlike methods. Editor Jim Casada's collection, *America's Greatest Game Bird: Archibald Rutledge's Turkey-Hunting Tales*, recaptures this time period. The fall and winter hunting tradition is ever-present in these works.

Such traditions can be geographically specific, of course. For example, records show that my native Pennsylvania made spring hunting illegal in 1873 (until that point even spring hens incubating eggs were free for the killing), closing turkey season from the New Year through October first. Then, and even nearly a century later when I first hunted Keystone State turkeys, the prevailing notion was that calling spring birds into range was easier due to the mating season, and arguable or not, that fall hunting was the true challenge. (For those of us who hunt both seasons nowadays, this assertion surely depends on the particular turkey we're dealing with at the moment.)

The rich tradition of American call making flourished during the early to mid-twentieth century, and calling turkeys was indeed perfectly legal in many places—even as turkey numbers continued to decline in

Classic books such as McIlhenny/Jordan's **The Wild Turkey and Its Hunting** *and Henry E. Davis's* **The American Wild Turkey** *reflect the fall and winter turkey-hunting tradition.*

some parts of our country. Names like Jordan, Turpin, and Gibson are part of call making history, among others. Many of our modern manufactured calls are modeled after their original examples.

Elsewhere, chance encounters using woodsmanship to find autumn turkeys was the prevailing tactic in places like Pennsylvania, where calling turkeys was deemed illegal in 1923. Their fall season was also pushed to November 1, and sunrise-to-sunset hours were set in place to end nighttime roost shooting. Turkey populations were also sustained during this time by the mountainous, difficult-to-hunt geography. Decades later, calling Keystone State turkeys was again legalized.

By the 1940s, Alabama call maker M. L. Lynch began traveling to market his now-famous box calls to interested parties. In fact, my father purchased one in the mid-1950s at the downtown Emporium, Pennsylvania, gas station where the road-tripping Lynch sold calls out of his pickup truck. Rich with personal meaning and turkey hunting history, the box call (one of the last of the Mike Lynch-decorated versions) sits nearby behind glass as I type this. It's interesting to note that in Lynch's time, turkey hunting was only permitted in fifteen states, as opposed to a generous forty-nine now in the spring and forty-three states in the fall and/or winter.

Once outlawed in some states, calling devices are now acceptable everywhere wild turkeys are hunted. Pictured here, Quaker Boy's late Wayne Gendron, a box-call specialist.

Calling devices are now acceptable everywhere wild turkeys are hunted—spring, fall, and winter. We'd be hard-pressed to find a turkey hunter without many calls among his personal possessions. Some of us have hundreds. In fact, a blended combination of calling tactics and savvy woodsmanship—first initiated long ago by Native Americans using wingbone callers—is largely viewed as the modern sporting way to take a wild turkey. It took awhile, but we got it right.

By 1968, spring hunting was legalized in Pennsylvania—a testament to rebounding turkey populations—though still viewed warily by some old-timers, as I remember. My dad recently noted that in the first few years of his spring turkey hunting in the late 1960s and early 1970s, it still felt like he was breaking the law. That's changed, too, as we've come to understand biology and viable management strategies. Nowadays, location depending, we can opt to hunt spring gobblers while protecting

By the early 1900s, the wild turkey was facing the same extinction that had eliminated the passenger pigeon. Today—thanks to sound game management—there are wild turkeys in forty-nine states (only Alaska has none), including parts of Canada, Mexico, and even Europe.

JOHN HAFNER PHOTO

nesting hens. In fall and winter, we can also target either-sex turkeys—both juveniles and adults—during a time when they've never been more abundant. Both traditions flourish. It's all turkey hunting.

States differ in their application of strategies, as the appreciation for hunting fall and winter birds varies from location to location. Some Pennsylvania ridge-runners still spot-and-shoot their fall turkey in likely autumn habitats with a rifle, using a combination of woodsmanship and marksmanship. Florida allows hunting for bearded birds only during this time. More than twenty states permit hunters to use dogs to find and flush flocks before setting up and then call those birds back to the blind. Some have liberal archery-only seasons that last for many months. Some limit it to specific zones or counties. Some, like Texas, offer a range of bow, firearms, and youth seasons on fall and winter turkeys. Several modern holdouts like Georgia and South Carolina have no autumn option, emphasizing spring gobbler management, while Indiana offered its first modern fall season in 2005. Options evolve as I write.

As a result, this handbook will cover the wide-ranging approaches and management perspectives inherent to this rich, ever-changing heritage. In the end, wild turkey flocks need ongoing attention to successfully offer varied, annual seasons. This balance is struck by noting harvest statistics (either real or estimated), hatch assessment, appropriate strategies, plus limited seasons and tags offered for the taking of birds. It's a fluid philosophy that affords spring, fall, and winter opportunities around our country as turkey numbers grow. There's something for everybody, and you can virtually hunt turkeys somewhere every month of the year but July and August. Things are looking pretty good these days for wild turkeys and hunters alike.

How good? According to the National Wild Turkey Federation (NWTF), there were just 1.3 million wild turkeys during the organization's founding year in 1973. Some 1.5 million sportsmen considered themselves turkey hunters back then. We've come a long way, friends. As of this writing, the NWTF—a pro-hunting, management-savvy organization with 525,000 members in fifty states and a dozen foreign countries—indicates seven million wild turkeys are available for roughly three million turkey hunters. Such good news makes for opportunity in the turkey woods fall, winter, and spring, location depending.

To hunt them, though, you first have to find them.

SOME WILD TURKEY FACTS

- By the early 1900s, the wild turkey was facing the same extinction that had eliminated the passenger pigeon. Today, thanks to sound game management, there are wild turkeys in forty-nine states (only Alaska has none), including parts of Canada, Mexico, and even Europe.

- Wild turkeys are extremely adaptable. When challenged, some Texas ranch Rio Grande turkeys will sleep on windmills and fences, while Eastern birds in urban areas have been seen loafing conveniently atop telephone poles and garage rooftops. Even sightings in NYC's Central Park have been documented.

- On average, wild turkeys live two to three years, but records indicate some banded birds have lasted as long as ten to twelve years.

- Some wild gobblers and hens exhibit the same smoky-gray to red-plumage color mutations as their domesticated cousins.

- A dominant spring gobbler is polygynous, meaning he breeds with as many hens as he can, without any future role in raising the hatched young through summer and into fall. The brood hen does that.

CHAPTER 2

Decode the mystery
of turkey movements
by studying the
ground they walked—
before, during, and
after the hunt.

Scouting Specifics

Scouting turkeys is a priority. Watching wild turkeys can be both an ongoing pleasure and a practical means of finding flocks when the season opens again. While some hunters may just scout right before opening day, regular study of turkey flocks not only yields better results, but also sustains interest year-round. During the season, scouting can help you make necessary adjustments when situations change.

THE BIRDS YOU HUNT
Turkeys roost and roam in a variety of locations across the United States. Subspecies include the Eastern, Osceola, Rio Grande, and Merriam's wild turkey, plus the Gould's and Ocellated south of the U.S. border (though Arizona also has a small Gould's population).

The Eastern subspecies of wild turkey lives in more than half of this geographical region, from Maine to Minnesota, Maryland to Missouri, and throughout the southern states, including small pockets in eastern Texas and the Plains states. Even Washington's Pacific Coast region now holds Easterns, as do areas of southern Canada along the U.S. border. This subspecies thrives in hardwood forests north to south. They favor agricultural landscapes with pastures and grassy glades near forested hills. There are often streams and creeks nearby, and roosting cover might accompany that running water. As long as food sources are available, fall and winter flocks are likely in the same locations you find birds in the springtime.

The Osceola, or Florida wild turkey, lives south of the panhandle. Hardwood hammocks near cypress swamps provide roosting cover in this peninsula region. Pinewoods, creek bottoms, open fields, and pastureland flanking wooded areas offer additional habitat. Expect to find

Scouting turkeys is a priority. Here, Kevin Evans glasses October fields for upstate New York fall flocks.

murky water, biting bugs, poisonous snakes, and toothsome gators in Osceola haunts. The Sunshine State is the only home to this subspecies. Though challenged by human development, public and private hunting opportunities still exist in central and southern Florida. Cattle ranches, if you can access permission there, often hold birds.

The Rio Grande subspecies thrives primarily in Texas and Oklahoma, while trap-and-transfer and subsequent flock growth of these birds has created populations in Kansas, Colorado, Utah, Nevada, California, Oregon, Washington, and elsewhere. Hawaii's turkeys are also Rio Grandes. Roosting cover—either natural in the form of live oaks, or manmade such as powerline structures—hold birds. Big Lone Star State ranches, which offer pay-as-you-go turkey hunting, hold large numbers of Rios.

The Merriam's wild turkey yelps and gobbles over a variety of habitats. This nomadic subspecies is found in coniferous hills and mountains of the West, river bottoms, canyon flats, and in semiarid desert cover. Depending on their location, Merriam's favor ponderosa pine roosts and cottonwoods. As with other subspecies, nearby water sources are required. Montana, Idaho, Wyoming, South Dakota, Colorado, New Mexico, and Arizona have good populations. As subspecies go, Merriam's flocks travel widely between roosting trees to feeding zones and are often highly visible at a distance.

Finally, hybrid forms of the wild turkey inhabit North Dakota, Nebraska, Kansas, and Oklahoma, plus parts of Oregon and Utah. The Gould's subspecies is found over the Mexican border (and in extreme southern Arizona), where it roosts in scrub oaks and big pines in semiarid mountainous ranges. The exotic Ocellated wild turkey, a bit on the outside range of this writer's personal radar, inhabits the Yucatan Peninsula. In the end, though, they're all turkeys, and that's what we like to hunt.

TURKEYS THROUGH THE SEASONS

In all honesty, I am as interested in encountering hens during the spring hunt as chasing vocal gobblers with a tag still left in my wallet. A female turkey whose aggressive territorial dominance you challenge with your own bold hen yelping might pull a strutting tom into gun or bow range as it waddles on in behind her. That same hen might nest nearby and lay a clutch of eggs later on. This is where an autumn flock will likely linger come late September and beyond.

It's all connected. As days subtly begin to draw shorter toward autumn, what you saw back in spring reveals itself. You spot a flock for the first time near a nesting site. You see that the gobbler you couldn't kill in spring is still alive come fall. It's a mystery rivaling anything popular culture might dish out. For the year-round wild turkey hunter, there's never any quitting involved. The seasons are seamless: sometimes you carry a gun or bow, sometimes you don't. But you're always thinking about turkeys.

Before their young hatch, the nesting hens' home range is obviously limited. I've seen them ground nesting in relatively sparse cover near busy back roads or deep in the shadowy woods. Not surprisingly, I regularly find hens where I've hunted spring gobblers a month or two before. On such chance occasions, I've watched them out of the corner of my eye as I've passed by, trying not to indicate they've been seen. Often the bird will hold tight and remain on her nest. Other times the brood hen will wait until she thinks she's been spotted, then suddenly flee—either on foot or by taking wing. If I unintentionally bump her in this dramatic manner, I stay out of her territory until a sufficient amount of time has passed, and I know the birds have likely hatched and are roosting in trees. One sighting is enough for now.

During this time, I periodically watch for the first appearance of brood hens with their newly hatched young. Depending on the location and particular nesting turkey, I've seen poults first appear as early as the ongoing spring season while chasing May gobblers, and even mid to late summer with certain delayed hatches. I've simultaneously spotted family flocks in an area where the juveniles in one group are twice as large as the young birds in another. Some are pheasant-sized. Some rival quail.

Again, you should be cautious about putting too much pressure on nesting hens or recently hatched broods. Still, it doesn't hurt to get an early sense of the potential hatch in the areas you hunt. Time will reveal much more.

While some may speak in generalized terms of the hatch being comprehensively early or late, dismissively bad or overly good, in truth hatching poults—emerging from eggs in the laying order, biology tells us—hatch over a broad window of time. Once started, an entire clutch hatches in several days. Anyone who goes outdoors regularly looking for turkeys will note this. This is why some ragged-feathered, pimple-spurred jakes with cigar-stub beards might be taken a year later during the following spring, while other juvenile males tagged then have nearly full fans, five bearded inches on their chests, and peaked but not-quite-pointed spurs. Early hatch. Late hatch. That's the difference.

Avoid oversimplifying your perspective related to the number of turkeys hatched that spring and summer. Stay positive. Chances are you haven't even come close to seeing them all.

Midsummer is the time period that some turkey hunters puzzle over. Will the recent weather, maybe a prolonged spring rain with chilling cold, affect the hatch? Do you have reason to worry about not seeing evidence of local birds? The only way to know is to get out there and poke around. You simply cannot completely understand what's going on in the woods by watching from the road. Steering-wheel speculation is initially limited in scope, though increasingly rewarding as flocks begin to appear in fields as autumn approaches. It's easier to spot young birds as they grow.

On a casual basis, you can rise early and go for a daybreak hike in the area you might plan to hunt that fall. Binoculars in hand, you can note when and where you encounter a summer brood bobbing along like wind-up toys behind the mama hen. As veteran turkey hunters know, these birds need food, water, and sheltering roosts to get along in the wild. Food sources shift seasonally and can be identified as you scout. For newly hatched broods, bugging in woodlots, fields, or along edge cover is common. The hen leads them there, and there the poults learn to fend for themselves under her example, hunting insects the way she does. Escape cover usually isn't far away.

Later, identifying the flock's seasonal food needs will also come in handy, as these shift from summer into autumn and winter. Water needs, also provided by moisture in the insects they consume, and the need for overnight roosting cover are also important.

Again, chances are turkeys have hatched, even if you haven't found them yet. Those flocks may be keeping to the cooler woods instead of hitting the sun-bright fields. Keep at your scouting, and avoid any generalized perspectives based on how many or how few turkeys you've found—at least until August or September when some flocks should be more visible.

In my summertime and early fall scouting experience, Eastern summer family flocks can have home ranges consisting of a small woodlot to a thousand acres or more, especially if ridge tops, hillsides, river bottoms, dairy farms, and agricultural areas converge. Florida's Osceolas navigate piney woods, pastures, and creek bottoms paired with cypress swamps (where they often roost), and cover similar ground. Merriam's wild turkeys in mountainous Western habitats and Rio Grande flocks in Texas can have even more expansive home ranges. All subspecies keep on the move, as young turkeys are voracious and grow fast.

Landscape features can dictate how the brood hen maneuvers her charges, but invariably they move daily to find food. Poults can fly at ten days or so, and if you happen to encounter birds that don't, they've just been hatched. Those that alight in trees or low-lying bushes on the flush have been around a little while. At two weeks, they begin roosting in trees.

They gain size fast, these broods, and time in the wild sharpens their wariness. I've been almost perversely pleased in the past when a family flock I patterned suddenly changes its routine in late summer, maybe owing to a shift in food sources or some other unknown factor. It's then that finding sign in the form of tracks, droppings, dusting areas, molted feathers, and scratchings becomes important. Focusing on these details allows the fall turkey hunter to analyze the situation and piece the puzzle together as autumn approaches, when you start counting calendar days until the season opener.

TURKEY SIGN

A casual observer might think that a person scouting for turkey sign has lost something on the ground, but really he's trying to decode the mystery left behind by invisible birds that once moved through that area.

Tracks: Of all the ground-sign clues available, tracks are fairly common and are sometimes widely distributed given the landscape. Study the ground in places that might bear evidence: funnels from roosts to fields, muddy pasture edges, roadbeds, fence lines where birds travel, and so on. You might just find one track, but that's a start. Look around in the general area and you might note several more. Areas where birds feed often reveal their footprints. Check out water sources and any place you find mud, sand, or bare ground.

Mature gobblers leave big tracks.

Family flock tracks in dried mud.

In Florida, Osceola footprints might be tattooed along a sandy pasture rim adjacent to a cypress swamp. In Texas, you might note Rio Grande turkey tracks near a water source or broadcast feeder. Game trails might hold them most everywhere. Later on, well into winter, it might be a recent snow that tells the story for the Merriam's and Eastern subspecies.

Adult turkey toes are several inches long and point forward with the exception of the short hind toe, which balances this big bird. Mixed track sizes suggest a family group. Mature gobblers, and so-called "super jakes" (male turkeys born the spring of the previous year), leave big-footed examples as they roam alone or together in all-male groups in summer, fall, and into winter. You might also find tracks that indicate a solitary broodless hen or a group of female turkeys.

Study the tracks. Are they fresh? Old? Big? Small? Gobbler tracks are larger than hen tracks. Autumn juvenile turkeys have smaller track sizes based on age, and some late-hatch flocks reflect this.

As a traveling observer of these tracks, I've noted that Florida turkeys have slightly smaller footprints than those of other subspecies, and that some Pennsylvania and Wyoming mountain turkeys have thicker toes. Young turkeys have slender toe tracks when compared to those of adult

Turkey dropping on an October maple leaf.

birds. Instinctively, veteran turkey chasers can tell the difference, and if in doubt, finding a turkey track is almost as good as sexing birds. A turkey is a turkey is a turkey. One might mean more are nearby. Again, instinct and experience will combine to tell you what you are seeing.

A reader of one of my magazine articles once e-mailed me a question related to the average distance between the stepping footprints of a walking gobbler (I kid you not). He wanted to know the step length of a calmly walking tom as opposed to one that was running. His goal was to cover his truck with turkey track decals, one for each bird he'd harvested. His plan was to have those tracks walk all over his truck. He aimed for authenticity. It's either a blessing or a curse, but I had the answer.

I told him that when walking unhurried, wild turkeys—both gobblers and hens—make tracks roughly one foot apart. When running, I told him, turkeys stride about two feet or more. He said he'd send a photo of the truck, but I haven't seen it yet—though I still wonder how many turkey kills it would take to cover a pickup. In the end, if the tracks are twelve inches or so apart, the turkey that made them was walking. If the stride is bigger, it was definitely running from something—maybe you—or to something, possibly other turkeys.

Droppings: In addition to either standing, walking, or running tracks, look for the droppings turkeys leave on their daily rounds. Fecal matter confirms a turkey's presence as either recent or days and weeks before. Are these droppings moist on a dry day? Are they dried and falling apart? Generally, we speak of a gobbler dropping as being J-shaped, like a stubbed-out cigarette, and of the hen leavings as being round, firm, tightly curled, and bulbous. Many droppings bear the chalk white smudge of uric

TURKEY SIGN MADE SIMPLE

Hunters use the term "sign" to speak of one or many examples of evidence left behind by the quarry they're hunting.

- Damp droppings say turkeys were there recently.
- When slightly dispersed, concentrated feathers can indicate a roost site. When tightly compacted in a small area, they are evidence of a predator kill.
- Mixed sets of new and old tracks indicate flocks use the area regularly.
- Raked areas in the woods, along field edges, or in food plots often designate turkey feeding zones.
- Track size can reveal the sex and age of turkeys.
- Lots of sign indicates bigger flocks, while spare evidence reflects fewer numbers.
- Dusting bowls are fresh if the soil is loose and if other sign in them or nearby is new.
- Old sign may mean turkeys have left the area for other food sources.

acid produced from digested protein (often insects), while the rest of it is vegetative or miscellaneous matter. This distinction can lead you to where they've been feeding.

Time afield will also show you that droppings sometimes vary. Hens can also leave J-shaped droppings, and gobblers might defecate indefinable evidence. I've seen fresh droppings beneath the known roost of a single adult tom turkey that resembled the criteria for hens, and vice-versa. It's rarely mentioned elsewhere, but I've also noted wet dark-green splats dropped by roosting turkeys that are not nearly as recognizable as either the typical J-shaped or rounded and tightly-curled forms.

As with tracks, identify turkey droppings with studious clarity if possible. A nesting hen that rises just once a day to feed and defecate will often drop a chunky, piled-up blob. I've found such leavings when scouting in late spring and early summer—the first indication a sitting hen is somewhere nearby, and that her efforts are about to be rewarded (predators and cold spring weather be damned) with a hatching clutch.

During this phase, I tend to simply note (either in my journal or by casual thought) where I might bump an afternoon hen feeding on a field

Dusting areas reveal shallow depressions where turkeys roll belly-down in loose soil or sand. Here, a Merriam's hen is caught in the act. JOHN HAFNER PHOTO

edge. I might make distinctions between fresh droppings and old. If I'm in a particularly detail-oriented mode, I might possessively scuff out sign I encounter if only to notice when fresh droppings appear again. I might even pocket molted feathers. Subculturist? Quirky? Extreme scout gone over the edge? Guilty, guilty, and guilty.

During the actual hunting season, you don't usually have to determine the sex of turkeys since both gobblers and hens are often legal in fall and winter. You might only be able to tell with actual visual sightings. Sometimes it's enough to have found generic turkey droppings.

My grade-school daughter and I once watched a television show where the program's host held turkey droppings in the palm of his gloved hand. "Is that turkey poop?" Cora queried, half-awed, half-surprised. "Yup," I responded. "What would he want to do that for?" she offered. The subject of turkey droppings isn't for everyone.

Dusting areas: Signposts of activity, tracks, and droppings may lead you to areas where turkeys dust. These dusting areas are shallow depressions where hens and gobblers have rolled belly-down in the loose soil or sand. It's speculated that this warm-weather behavior is aimed at cooling birds, or theoretically to rid turkeys of parasites. Dirt roads, river edges, and the soft soil surrounding conifers may hold them. While watching birds in spring, summer, and early fall, I've noted that particular flocks often use such places predictably on the clock—often before or after feeding.

In the past I've used my knowledge of dusting areas to target fall flocks. During New Hampshire's three-month, archery-only season, I've found dusting late summer and early fall turkeys to show a regular pattern, visiting these spots at a certain time each day. Invariably this dusting activity continues as long as the ground soil stays loose and warm, which might be year-round depending on where you live.

In Vermont, while hunting turkeys with one of my English setters (a legal fall strategy there), we once found a flock of adult gobblers on top of a remote big-woods knob. Arriving at the flush site before setting up for the call back, I found tracks, droppings, and feathers in numerous dusting bowls that had obviously been used over and over again. From Maine to Wyoming, Texas to Missouri, and Kentucky to Florida, I've noted these locations. Finding such dusting areas where turkeys loaf helps piece the puzzle together.

Feathers: In spring, hunters might encounter fresh feathers that have been left after a gobbler has been shot or missed, or if a predator has been involved. Ever see a gobbler or hen without a tail? I have. That's what's happened. The coyote got the fan but not the bird, or maybe two gobblers

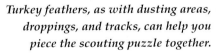

Turkey feathers, as with dusting areas, droppings, and tracks, can help you piece the scouting puzzle together.

squared off to establish the daily pecking order and lost several feathers. Feather evidence varies in volume.

Older feathers leftover from the previous season are weathered and faded. Fresh feathers found in summer and fall are most often recently molted. Dusting areas almost always contain a few breast feathers. Hen breast feathers are brown-edged, while those of gobblers are black-rimmed. Feathers of various sizes in a general area can indicate a family flock. Shed feathers dispersed widely beneath likely roosting trees show that a turkey flock is using that area.

Many feathers in a singularly tight group usually reveal a predator kill (I've seen this numerous times where summer poults are concerned). By noting what kinds of feathers you're finding, you can determine whether it's a family flock or if it's composed of adult gobblers or brood-less hens. Sometimes you find solitary birds this way.

Driven by my collecting mentality, I often reach down to keep the first molted feathers I find each summer. These might ride stashed in my truck's sun visor or get placed somewhere near my writing desk in a mug with pens and pencils. Molting continues through the autumn season and provides sure evidence that turkeys are around. Take notice, and match this sign with tracks, droppings, and dusting areas to pattern birds and to get a sense of where you might find them, in season or out.

Scratchings: These marks reveal where wild turkeys have been feeding. They scratch leaves to uncover hidden food sources, such as insects or plant tubers. You might see scratchings where food-plot chufa is planted or acorns have dropped. These rounded, upturned areas are often widely dispersed when a big flock moves through the area. Darker, damper soil exposed in the dry woods might indicate they moved through recently. General assumptions about the number of scratchings can indicate flock size or if you've just struck evidence of a single bird.

If you've ever watched turkeys feed this way, it's an animated deal. The bird reaches one foot forward then pulls it back, makes follow-up scratches with the other foot, and finally resumes with the initial lead foot. After the ground is exposed, the turkey studies it for something to eat. Robot-like, they'll move forward to do it again. Tracks, droppings, nearby dusting areas, and molted feathers may also be found in this home range. From pre-season to opening day, it pays to keep track of the shifting signs.

SCOUTING PHILOSOPHY

For me, pre-season, in-season, and post-season turkey scouting is a pleasurable activity. It might involve studying birds in my home region, and transferring this know-how to turkeys I hunt elsewhere in the fall. Once learned, this knowledge of flock behavior might then be used during a

Scratchings, pictured here, reveal where turkeys have been feeding.

road trip where I'm new to the area and have to gain a quick understanding of the immediate situation. Turkeys share common behavior, and spending time with them reveals these traits.

A phone call to a landowner can provide a great deal of information. So can a conversation with someone who doesn't hunt birds but who has seen them. To me, this year-round compulsive activity of watching, scouting, and talking about turkeys can't be underestimated. I'm interested in watching and hunting turkeys year-round, and if you're reading this book, you probably are, too.

Now true enough, you can hunt wild turkeys fall, winter, or spring by simply dialing up a reliable guide service and hiring a person who has been watching and actively scouting birds. That's fine, of course. You're purchasing that person's scouting time and effort. Over the years I've enjoyed hunts with folks who put me into flocks they knew about. In turn, I have also put friends into turkeys I'd found and studied (just short of naming them). It's all good. The first step is to note the daily travels of a particular brood hen or hens with their newly hatched young after the spring season closes, then build your understanding from there.

All this scouting is a continuum, an attitude, a philosophy of paying attention to turkeys year-round. In season or out, it's beneficial to study the evidence turkeys leave behind. To hunt and scout birds, though, you first need access to land and habitat that is likely to hold them. Some of it might be state-owned or left unposted by a hunter-friendly landowner. Negotiations might be required.

Keeping a simple but detailed scouting journal allows you to assess information you're finding when afield before the season, during, and after it. In my case such a notebook allows me to make notes, then relax. The pages will remember for me.

Time and again, I've casually read through such notes and a hunt plan has come together for me. Important details such as weather, time of day, hours hunted or scouted, and location—including hand-drawn maps—can help you hunt better. I also keep a list of turkey flock sightings volunteered by hunting buddies, but more often by people who don't hold the same passion for these birds that I do.

You might note the ground sign you've found, and the wild turkey calls you've heard. You can even list other important information such as season dates, flock movement theories, the patterning of turkey loads and the results, and landowner phone numbers or e-mail addresses. You can list the vital statistics of birds you kill during the season—and of course your glorious misses—plus flock breaks your turkey dog succeeds in making.

Carry this notebook in your vehicle, your jacket pocket, or keep it on your desk at home. Record entries the moment you get in the door while impressions are fresh or outdoors as you scout.

Even when you figure out what the turkeys are doing, that situation can change when other hunters locate the same birds. Always pay attention to who is scouting the same area—especially if it's public land—then plan accordingly. Other options need to be explored. Refer to your scouting journal for possibilities. Sometimes a long walk on a ridge top to find backwoods turkeys is better than the competitive scene several hundred yards from a country road where flocks have been noted by passing traffic.

CHAPTER 3

Key contacts help you hunt posted land for some of the best opportunities around for unpressured birds. After all, not all of us can be married to the farmer's favorite daughter.

Hunter Access

The Vermont farmer eyed me from his just-silenced tractor. "Open the gate, and come on in," he summoned, no doubt wanting to look me over. To him, I was pesky as a deer fly, a stranger stealing precious time. To me, he was my last hope at scoring on a distant road trip, so I moseyed on over.

I introduced myself and explained that I wrote about the outdoors, and then suddenly realized that this fact might definitely make him say no. I assured him I wouldn't provide explicit directions to his family farm in print for the hunting world to see, and then I noticed a faint smile. I also said I was only looking to hunt the next morning. You see, that late afternoon I'd glassed a flock of pasture turkeys from the dirt road that ran past his big property. Hard-pressed to find birds until that point, and more than three hours from home with a short window of hunting time, he must have seen a mix of desperation and hope in my eyes. But for a few minutes, he made me sweat.

"Saw you drive by in your truck a couple times," he deadpanned, "and figured you wanted something." Right then I was every other hunter who had ever asked for his permission.

"Ran a guy off yesterday," he hissed, looking away in the direction where I'd seen the flock of birds. "Seems he couldn't read the signs. Not sure which part of 'No Hunting' he didn't understand."

I listened, nodding. Now I was every guy who had trespassed on his place. I almost wanted to apologize.

"You seem okay though," he offered, glancing at my business card. "Most guys don't ask, they just come on in here like they own the place. I'll let you hunt, sure. Park up there by the gate. If you take a shot, make sure you do it with the cows in mind. And let me know how you do."

His faith in me was all I needed. Days after returning home, I let him know I'd met with success. During our conversation, he'd indicated his grandson did a little fly fishing. A book I'd written on the subject had appeared the year before, so I sent it to him, enclosing instructions to pass it along, with best wishes and added thanks in the note for the opportunity to hunt his place.

Such experiences are gifts, and turkey hunters rely on them routinely. Show gratitude whenever possible in such situations.

Places I hunt are often a patchwork of public and private properties. Turkey flocks don't know this of course, and roam widely, seeking out shifting autumn and winter food sources. Birds that have wandered onto private land can be hunted. You just have to approach the right person or persons and secure access. Here's how you might try.

READ THE SIGNS

Posted properties have sometimes received people pressure, though reasons for denying access might vary. Property abuse, whether you like to admit it or not, may have occurred at the hands of negligent sportsmen or other individuals using the area. Maybe ATVs have been run through there with reckless regularity. Maybe litter has been strewn about. Maybe

Read the signs. Hunter access is a privilege.

shots have been fired too close to dwellings or near livestock. Maybe the farmer has found one too many lost arrow shafts and broadheads while haying. Maybe outdoorsmen aren't to blame, but a few individuals who party there at night, leaving empty cans and other debris at makeshift backwoods fire rings along game trails. Whatever the reason, these poster-framed properties are sending a message to the world: you are not wanted here.

Sometimes these signs might indicate you have some hope: HUNT-ING BY PERMISSION ONLY. Sometimes posters might be generic and direct: HUNTING, FISHING, OR TRESPASSING FORBIDDEN FOR ANY REASON. Sometimes signs might be threatening: VIOLATORS WILL BE PROSECUTED TO THE FULL EXTENT OF THE LAW, or TRESPASSERS WILL BE SHOT ON SIGHT (SURVIVORS WILL BE SHOT AGAIN). I once saw a menu board of sorts bordering a farm that listed the individual cost of livestock if accidentally shot by you, the hunter. Signs hint at what kind of person you are dealing with. Read the detail there. It may offer a way to approach the landholder.

If the signs are new and nailed to every other fencepost, something bad has gone down, and it might be fresh as a wildfire in the mind of the landowner. Then again, maybe the land has just changed hands. Maybe the property holder feels it's easier not to risk having armed strangers around. If the signs are old, and torn or worn, it may no longer be officially posted. If signs are riddled with bird shot or several slug holes, chances are trouble has brewed there. You'll never know until you step up and ask.

Names and contact numbers should be listed on these posters, which can provide a direct link to information, so jot down these details in your scouting journal. Other times such signs are left blank, as if the landowner wants to convey the message that visitors aren't wanted, and that they don't wish to be contacted about the matter. Sometimes posters might also hang on properties where access isn't legally prohibited. They may have no right to post it.

"Just because our land isn't posted doesn't mean you have an invitation to hunt it," a landowner once said on an autumn road trip through upstate New York. Awkward or not, it is always best to ask permission even if the property seems ripe for hunting. On the other hand, in some states the use of private unposted land by the general public or state residents is a time-honored tradition. As an example, New England states such as New Hampshire offer longstanding public common-law access on non-posted land. Abuse it, though, and you can lose it. Once the posters go up, it ends. Game over. Do whatever you can to keep those orange and yellow signs from appearing.

Ironic or not, in some locations reverse-posting situations apply. If the land isn't posted for a specific use, you can't hunt it. Other states require landowner permission to hunt, whether the land is posted or not. Some turkey hunters routinely pay annual lease fees for using posted landowner-held property. It can be on a daily, weekly, or annual basis. Some pay a fee every time they take a bird there. I once dropped fifty bucks that way, but it was worth it.

Sometimes you can secure access directly, as I did with the Vermont farmer. Other times you may need an intermediary. This go-between person can be your goodwill ambassador, making subtle suggestions to the landowner.

Initially, contact with this intermediary might come accidentally. Off-site places and situations like roadside diners, town-meeting locations, grocery stores, yard sales, even Friday night at the local bar can provide the connection you need. You could run into a person who owns the property, or a neighbor who knows the people who do. You need to research the full ownership picture as that land is concerned. If you can't figure out who owns the land in this casual, conversational way, court-house records can be studied. Who really owns the land? Who really calls the shots? Is ownership fragmented? Is ownership in transition?

Sometimes this go-between person can introduce you to landowners who post their properties, especially if they're a person of good standing in the community. If lucky, they might accompany you to the location for a direct introduction, replete with small talk and handshakes to seal the deal. Sometimes that intermediary can simply call the landholder up and describe what vehicle you'll be driving. Arrive there cold, with out-of-state license plates during a road trip, and you might nullify any hope at gaining access. They can tell that property owner you'll be dropping by to say hello. They can determine where your vehicle should be parked. They can make your first visit to the posted place as comfortable as possible for the person granting you access. Imagine what it might be like for posted-property holders, and then do what you can to gain their trust.

Some of the best turkey hunters I know have key contacts like this, and they get to hunt posted land, which invariably holds some of the best opportunities around for unpressured birds. After all, not all of us can be married to the farmer's favorite daughter.

TIME IT RIGHT

If possible, seek permission in the off-season. If you're hunting a new location in the fall, try getting access during the summer months. Meet the landowner in street clothes, under relaxed circumstances rather than

Research the full ownership picture on properties you turkey hunt.

desperate. Have you seen a new family flock appear on a posted property by chance? Study the options for hunting there later. Let landowners know how you'll hunt, where you'll do it on the property, what you'll be doing in there, and who—if anyone—you'll bring along. Again, sometimes it's best to do so outside their home, so that they don't feel any undo pressure to say yes. Sometimes it's tougher to get permission during the ongoing hunting season. Show up in camouflage then, and it might strike them as an unexpected assault akin to a telemarketer's suppertime call, but with more longstanding, negative implications. Visit them wearing clean pants, a pressed shirt, and a smile on your mug, and you might pass the initial test. Image is sometimes everything. Sell yourself. Don't intimidate.

Though it might seem a little solicitous, you can also market yourself by running off a brochure at your local printing center or using computer software, which you can hand to them when you seek access. List your membership in certain conservation organizations. Record your professional credentials there. Indicate you've successfully passed a hunter's safety course. Mention your wife, kids, and even church affiliation if appli-

No matter how you eventually secure posted-land permission, do whatever you can in the off-season to show your thanks. If folks trust you on their land, keep that relationship going.

cable. Shape your image. Indicate you're serious about your turkey hunting, but also safety-minded. Sell yourself in advance of hunting there.

Sometimes, though, it is definitely not in your best interest to tell the landowner everything you're doing there. Keep it simple. Certain folks might not wish to hear every detail about how you eventually secure a turkey by the feet. You may love turkey hunting, but it isn't for everyone. Think about your audience. Don't lie to them, but if necessary, don't elaborate too much either.

Though this might run counter to previous suggestions, it might benefit you to offer to post land that is seeing undo negative pressure. Maybe a landowner has sought out your help in this matter. Selfish, surely, but you can sometimes stake claim over landholdings by doing so. Controversial or not, you can fashion out a niche and ensure yourself a nice little hunting property. It won't win you points with your buddies, but you can indicate to the landowner that only you will hunt there. Once you make this arrangement, never violate the promise. Even if your hunting pals routinely joke about how secretive you are about some of your spots, change the subject, or laugh it off.

And in the end, if the landowner does eventually change his or her mind and say no, pick your ego up off the ground, dust it off, and try again to secure posted-land access somewhere else. Truth told, it's just short of actually leasing the land for hunting purposes, but without the overhead.

GIVE THANKS

No matter how you eventually secure posted-land permission, do whatever you can in the off-season to show your thanks. If they trust you on their land, keep that relationship going. Offer to fix fences. Bale hay. Feed the livestock. Mow a lawn. Move silage. Whatever. Drop off a ham during the holidays. Call them up to touch base now and again. Offer them turkey breast from birds you take there. Keep that posted-land permission. Don't just ask what's in it for you. Even the score.

People are inherently skeptical of strangers, but in time you can become friends. To do so, be a good example. You're not just out there hunting for yourself. You represent all turkey hunters.

CHAPTER 4

The fascinating thing about these big highly vocal birds is that sometimes turkeys don't call at all. Here a silent gobbler walks into range.

JOHN HAFNER PH⊙

Turkey Vocabulary

Wild turkeys call to communicate in the wild, and almost any turkey sound the human hunter makes chances at luring a curious bird in for a look. Or not. That's the calling game. You need to interpret what you're hearing from live birds to successfully imitate them.

Turkeys communicate alarm at a predator's real or perceived presence and vocalize a sense of well being when all seems safe. Some thirty distinctions have been determined, while fewer than half of these are applicable as hunting calls. Some guys tag birds regularly with timely clucking. Others use as many calling strategies as possible. Either way, understanding the turkey's vocabulary can enhance your enjoyment of the fall and winter hunt.

Even if you don't use the range of available calls, hearing live birds afield can clue you in to what might happen next. It helps you think like a turkey.

CALLING ALL TURKEYS

Turkey poults begin calling before hatching. They communicate peeping sounds to their brood hen, who in turn softly yelps at the stirring life inside the eggs; again, all this before young turkeys peck out of their shells. On hatching, the young turkeys and adult hen can both identify the source of these vocalizations since their introduction has already been made. While scouting in summer you may hear a variety of turkey sounds—including those made by the brood hen to her charges, and vice-versa. These calls linger into hunting season, changing as the flock ages. This connection is strong, as the young turkeys need to honor the brood hen's instructions; their survival often depends on it.

Turkeys communicate alarm at a predator's real or perceived presence and vocalize a sense of well being when all seems safe. Some thirty call distinctions have been determined, but fewer than half of these are applicable for hunting.
JOHN HAFNER PHOTO

One summer while afield with a new pup—our English setter, Radar—I paused as he locked up on point where I doubted the presence of birds. I stepped forward, scanning the field grass, fully expecting a songbird to flush wildly, if anything. Though it's legal to train bird dogs year-round where I live, we weren't looking. Still, there he was on point—tail a feathery plume, body erect, eyes wide open in a stance that said "bird." I looked and saw nothing. My own human nose was of no help at all.

Right then a feathered dragon arose out of the weeds, scolding us with her wailing alarm, peeping poults briefly heard but not seen at her scaly feet. Head outstretched, the brood hen dropped her wings and rushed us. With my setter pup's checkcord in hand, we moved away, but not before the hen flew-hopped a few steps in the other direction, and moved in agitated semi-circles like a boxer in the ring. Curious to hear the hen recall her charges, I later listened from the dirt road where I'd parked. Soon came the sound of her insistent yelping, and the urgent whistling of the poults. They noisily regrouped, and as expected, went silent.

The hen's genetic desire to watch over her growing brood continues well into the autumn hunting season. As mentioned, this bond is a major factor in survival, and it's reflected in the hen's vocalizations as these birds mature. Fall and winter calling includes the brood hen's assembly yelp, along with the juvenile turkeys' kee-kee and kee-kee-run.

The assembly yelp: This turkey call is a variation on the plain, lost, and tree yelp, which I'll detail shortly. It's made by the brood hen either to gather the flock on the ground at morning fly-down time, or following the separation of brood members by a predator, including the human hunter. The six- to twelve-note assembly-yelp call—I've heard even more notes in some situations—draws the young turkeys to the brood hen from wherever they have been dispersed. Each hen is different. Some sound like yapping dogs. Some could win a calling contest. Nevertheless, each juvenile bird can identify the individual hen's voice, which makes it difficult to imitate the assembly yelp in a hunting situation, though occasionally you get lucky and call in the brood hen.

It's clear that brood bosses sometimes challenge other imposters in the woods. I've even seen autumn adult hens strut on several occasions in a posture of dominance. In this situation, it's often best to stand in sight and spook the brood hen to silence her—unless of course you want to legally take that bird. It's your decision in either-sex hunting situations, as always. If you choose to run her off, you can then imitate the calls of young turkeys, specifically the kee-kee and kee-kee-run, and pull one of those juvenile birds in.

The kee-kee and kee-kee-run: The kee-kee call is the maturing lost whistle of the young turkey transitioning in the fall. It's three notes and roughly two seconds long. The kee-kee-run includes these three notes, with yelps added on the end (that's the "run" part). Four to ten notes might compose the kee-kee-run, which is about six to seven seconds long. When separated from their flockmates and regrouping, young autumn gobblers will often call with a kee-kee-run, and a gobble tagged on the end. Some might kee-kee, yelp, gobble, kee-kee, and then yelp again in growing urgency. Calls vary.

Following their morning fly-down from the roost, or after being flushed by a predator, young turkeys often reassemble together first, then move in small groups to greet the hen as she makes assembly yelps. Highly talkative when lost, wild turkeys sometimes call repetitiously as they approach another vocal juvenile hen or gobbler. That's why, during a hunt, you can mimic a young turkey as it calls and pull that bird into range much easier than trying to imitate the brood hen.

As autumn hunters, we need to understand this family-flock language, and to interpret what it means when we hear vocalizations in the turkey woods. Even the turkey's yelp is multifaceted. Made year-round, the plain, lost, and tree yelp—like the brood hen's assembly yelps—are often specifically situational.

Plain yelping: This call is roughly three to eight notes long, and the calling option most often employed by spring turkey hunters to lure gobblers into range. As with other vocalizations, turkeys make it to indicate their position. The fall and winter hunter can hear it from individual birds, including those turkeys in broodless hen flocks, and all-male gobbler gangs. Hen yelping is higher-pitched than the deeper, coarser yelping of gobblers. Tom turkeys yelp with a slower cadence as well, and yelps are generally fewer in number (often three notes in my experience: yawp, yawp, yawp).

Lost yelps: Lost hen yelps are louder and longer in duration than plain yelps. When separated from flockmates, turkeys of either sex sometimes call with loud, repetitious vocalizations. I've heard lost yelping from scattered, broodless adult hen flocks in the fall many times. They call urgently until visual contact is made, then go silent on getting back together. Autumn gobblers will yelp and sometimes even gobble to indicate their location when separated.

Tree yelping: Tree yelps are made with a soft series of sounds when the turkey is on the morning roost. It seems to be used to determine the position of branch-sitting birds in the flock before fly-down time. Short in duration, hens usually make this call with three to five notes. Soft clucking might also be part of this initial calling to greet the new day. Male fall and winter turkeys may simply just gobble on the roost as they do in spring.

Cackling: This sound is made as the turkey rapidly wings down out of its roost tree and can range from several to nearly several dozen notes, depending on the distance the bird flies to hit the ground. Breaking branches as feather tips brush and claw through trees adds to the listening experience. It may even indicate the direction of flight to other birds— and to the human hunter.

Clucking: When looking for flockmates or other lone hens and gobblers, wild turkeys cluck. It's an effort to get another bird to step into view, and is made by a turkey as if to ask, "Where are you?" In an autumn or winter hunting situation, turkeys will often cluck on the approach, especially if you are clucking back, or even making another call. Gobbler clucks are often low-pitched when compared to a hen's. Clucks for both sexes can be spaced out, often two to three seconds or more between calls. Sometimes the bird might make just one. This sound may be soft or loud depending on the situation. Pitting, a kind of high-pitched clucking, can be heard if a predator, like you beneath them, disturbs the roosted flock.

To feed in a properly dispersed way, turkeys let flock members know their whereabouts by purring. JOHN HAFNER PHOTO

Purring: This call, which might range from soft to rather loud, reflects the turkey's level of tolerance and perhaps even irritation among other birds feeding or fighting. By analogy, it's like the soft, short growl of a dog bent over its food bowl when another nearby canine approaches. Dominance rules in the wild, and each situation might reflect it on a year-round basis. For turkeys to feed in a properly dispersed way in a woods full of acorns or a food plot full of chufa, they have to let each other know their whereabouts. Purring does this for gobblers and hens alike. Hunters cagily approaching an area might detect the presence of a fall flock by listening for it. In the turkey woods, you can hear a broad range of loud gobbling and soft purring; some calls are subtle, some shockingly loud.

Alarm putting: This sharp "pock" sound is made when the turkey detects the presence of possible danger. It's a call every turkey hunter has heard with the sinking of his or her heart. Like the cluck, it's used to get the attention of another bird. An uneven, single-note call, it broadcasts suspicion in the turkey woods. If you hear it in a once-silent situation, it means the turkey saw you before you detected it. An alarm putt might be a directive made by a brood hen to silence her juvenile flock as well. Poults also putt at a young age. As a call, it also seems to be directed to the predator, indicating the prey-hunting game is now momentarily over. Does it work? Ask yourself: how many times have you given up on that turkey after hearing it?

The cluck and putt are closely related. It's safe to say that a turkey looking for you and your calling position is clucking, while one that has just agitatedly flicked its wings and turned to walk away is putting.

Cutting: Also called loud clucking, this call is sometimes used by turkeys after fly-down, when the regrouping flock is on the ground but

Alarm putting. This sharp "pock" sound is made when the turkey detects the presence of possible danger. Since the cluck and putt are closely related, it's safe to say that a turkey looking for your calling position is clucking, while one that has just agitatedly flicked its wings and turned to walk away is putting. JOHN HAFNER PHOTO

still visually separated. At times, cutting is made by one calling turkey as it stands in place, while another insistently yelping bird approaches its position. The lost turkey often goes to the stationary bird, which may be in a flock. Sometimes the group of birds may move to meet the solitary turkey, too. Many turkey hunters have called up cutting hens to their position by mimicking the calls of that fired-up bird. Sometimes you can interest a hen or gobbler with your enthusiastic calling. This chances at bringing the whole flock toward you. At least you've possibly identified some huntable turkeys if one answers you this way. Gobbling can be like that, too.

Gobbling: This easily recognized call can be heard early in the New Year as weather warms in the nation's Snow Belt. This pre-mating period in winter foreshadows the time when hens are ready to breed. The gobble is a call to gather hens for breeding, though I've also seen and heard spring, fall, and winter gobblers locate each other this way. Later on, even as breeding time passes and hens begin to nest, gobbling continues. It can linger well into late spring and early summer in some parts of the country. In my experience afield—whether it be conditioning my bird dogs in summer, or simply being outdoors where turkeys live—gobbling can be heard from January to June, and on slate-colored November days. Basically, it's a year-round call, with peaks and valleys.

Between the gobbler's anticipation of spring breeding season, and the intense urge to establish pecking order with male birds on an almost daily basis, gobblers call year-round in varying degrees of intensity. Strutting gobblers in fall and winter spit and drum just as they do in spring—a "pfft, dummm" sound. This is a close-range call that other turkeys chance at hearing if in range.

One southern Maine Thanksgiving week not long ago, with the temperature just above freezing, I glassed a large flock of wild turkeys in a pasture corner. The mega-group of birds consisted of brood hens, juvenile turkeys, and three full-fan strutters. Quite the sight, that was. Clearly they were grouped together in pre-winter mode: family flocks and adult gobblers alike, with the toms jostling for pecking order, and the young birds feeding with the brood hens.

In hunting situations, I've also heard intense autumn and winter gobbling while calling all-male turkey flocks back after scattering them. I defy any turkey hunter to tell me this isn't just as exciting as what the spring hunt might offer. Fixed on the flush site, and drawn to it by the calling of other members of that gang of toms and/or jakes, gobbling coming from all directions on the approach to your setup is hard to beat on the intensity level. They cluck. They yelp. They make a wonderful racket at times.

While some spring hunters rely almost entirely on the gobble to locate male turkeys and then scratch their heads when birds shut down and go silent, the fall and winter enthusiast must listen for the range of turkey sounds in the woods—assuming the birds are talking.

The fascinating thing about these big highly vocal birds is that sometimes turkeys don't call at all. On some occasions, you might just hear them fly down in the morning, and wing up to roost at night. In such situations, woodsmanship—and noting tracks, droppings, and other sign on the ground—will help you find silent birds. I've called up fall turkeys that have never answered back by knowing that they were somewhere near, though tight-beaked. Individual turkeys may also softly cluck or yelp nearby at hearing your footsteps in the leaves—a muted effort, perhaps, to identify the approaching noise, and draw a response from the maker of that sound.

In the end, you need to actively listen while scouting and hunting to distinguish isolated turkey sounds from other outdoor noises. Between the desire of wild turkeys to stay alive, an urgency reflected in many of their calls, and the gregariousness of these birds wishing to get together, a range of vocalizations might be heard in the autumn and winter woods and fields where flocks roam. The best path of study is to get out there and listen for them.

CHAPTER 5

Listen for footsteps in the leaves or snow, especially after you've made some initial contact with turkeys or suspect one is close.

JOHN HAFNER PHOTO

Listen Up

Some springtime sportsmen rely almost entirely on the male turkey's gobble to initiate a hunt. Without it, they're lost. Talk of quiet birds can dominate pre-dawn breakfasts from Mississippi to Maine, souring taste buds in a way no camp cook's hearty breakfast could ever fix. That's too bad. The tom turkeys are still out there.

Gobble or no gobble, fall and winter enthusiasts need to translate a diverse range of sounds into meaningful information for locating flocks and individual turkeys they want to pursue. While springtime sportsmen would certainly benefit by diversifying their listening strategies when afield, the woodstove-month hunter depends on it. Some sounds to listen for involve vocal turkeys, as detailed in the previous chapter. Some include non-calling noises that indicate hens and gobblers are nearby.

Cut the engine. Step out, and close the truck door slowly so it quietly snaps shut. Take a deep breath. Slow down. No, this isn't yoga instruction, but you can't go stomping into the woods and hear turkeys effectively. To listen well, you've got to move along slowly and surely, attentive and calmly focused. If possible, ignore the vehicular traffic on the distant highway. Turn your cell phone off. You may note the humming of early-season field insects and crows cawing overhead. Relax. Now listen for the sounds within this outdoor noise to hear the quarry you're after.

Approach likely habitats such as fields, old clearcuts, power lines, and ridges from a downwind position to better hear. You might catch the purring of feeding birds and other soft calling this way. On excessively windy days, focus your attention on river bottoms and draws where flocks can get out of the blowing gusts and you can hear more clearly.

To listen well, you have to be quiet yourself. Alone, it's not too hard. When buddy hunting, it's tougher. Keep small talk to a minimum. You may miss sounds you need to hear to hunt effectively. When listening for turkeys at fly-down time with a friend, move some distance away, and sit apart. Do the same thing when birds are flying up to roost. One of you may pick up noises or see something the other person doesn't. The sounds you hear in the woods tell a story.

Squirrels routinely bark at turkeys passing nearby, scolding the movement of most any creature in the woods beneath their treetop views. Listen for these squirrels acting agitated, especially if you suspect a turkey is on the approach. Crows call loudly in the presence of flocks as well, and even dive-bomb at groups of birds when asserting territorial dominance. This harassment is curious to the naturalist and hunter and might happen for a variety of reasons. Sometimes the cawing interlopers gather in tree-held groups above turkeys. Turkeys and crows seem to have a long history of being annoyed with each other. I've seen wild turkeys chase crows out of fields. At breeding time, crows certainly raid brood hen nests. And it's no secret to spring enthusiasts that a crow call can be used to draw shock gobbles from male turkeys as a means of locating them. I've had

To listen well, you've got to move along slowly and surely, attentive and calmly focused.

Wings slam and pop. Chests collide in a show of strength. Leaves rustle as turkeys jostle for position. Welcome to the daily fight for pecking order, which often comes right after gobblers gather after fly-down. JOHN HAFNER PHOTO

both squirrels and crows indicate the nearby presence of turkeys on hunts around the country. Blue jays and other birds sometimes grow agitated when turkeys are near too. Active listening helps piece together the turkey hunting puzzle.

Wings slam and pop. Chests collide in a show of strength. Leaves rustle as turkeys jostle for position. Welcome to the daily fight for pecking order, which often comes right after male birds land on their feet after fly-down. A gobbler brawl can sound like two kickboxers sparring in the ring. Their big wings slap, and their reptilian necks twist. Their beaks peck and throats purr, with their feet and spurs in the air, as other turkeys look on. Even hens contest for rank within a flock. You can listen for it and often pinpoint the direction of the group's movements. I've heard these fights on numerous occasions during hunts, even when the turkeys weren't calling much.

What do you do when turkeys are silent, or they aren't calling loud enough to hear, but you know they might be nearby? Listen for footsteps in the leaves or snow, especially after you've made some initial contact with birds or suspect one is close. Safety rules, as always. Footsteps that approach your position could be a squirrel, a turkey, or maybe another

Turkey hunting is a game of listening well. Here Woods Wise's Gary Sefton zeroes in on nearby sounds.

hunter. Err on the side of caution. Make a final visual confirmation of the sounds you hope will materialize into a turkey. In addition to footsteps made while walking, leaf scratching might signal that turkeys are feeding nearby. Soft purring (a close-range sound), which often accompanies that activity, will confirm it. Depending on how close they are, you can either call to the birds, reposition on them, or wait for the turkeys to possibly ease within shot range.

Make a mental inventory of the wild game that's in season if you hear a gunshot. In spring, it's often at a gobbler, or perhaps at a coyote that wandered in to turkey sounds, or somebody target shooting nearby. In fall and winter, it could be a range of game birds and animals, rifle or shotgun depending. Either way, if you think that gun blast was made by a fall or winter turkey hunter, stay put. Scattered birds might wander into your area. You might also be able to call up a single bird that's been dispersed from the noise of the shot.

If a buddy is on the next ridge, and likely took a bird (or tried to), sit tight. You might be able to celebrate together with your own turkey in hand. By all means, such hunters should work out a system of meeting up again during a hunt. Safety demands it. By no means should you ever make turkey calls as you approach his position. That's a no-brainer, right? You can regroup by owl hooting on the approach, or using another bird or animal sound readily identifiable to your friend. Sometimes it just makes sense to whistle. Walkie-talkies (where legal) or cell phones (service providing) can hook you up, but again, these devices inhibit listening abilities.

Hearing-enhancement devices can assist in locating both calling and non-calling turkey sounds. It goes without saying that the shooting sports damage listening abilities. To hunt well, though, you need to recoup losses. Consider using some of the technical aids on the market, especially during the active-listening part of the hunt. If you're a wing shooter or waterfowler when not turkey hunting and habitually take a lot of shots, wear protective earplugs on those occasions. Turkey hunting is a game of listening well, and you can't do it as effectively with appreciable hearing loss.

If a gobble is the most easily recognizable sound in the turkey woods for some, the cluck is a subtle call you might unintentionally miss. As you ease through the woods and along field edges, try to distinguish all the many noises. When you hear something that sounds like a cluck, stop. Listen. It may be a turkey asking for you to respond. So do it.

CHAPTER 6

Wingbone calls
connect traditionalist
hunters with call
making history.

Calling Turkeys

There is no strategy quite as satisfying as calling a bird into range. After all, you've successfully
spoken turkey as a second language and fooled a real gobbler or
hen into thinking you're one, too.

Humility often masks talent. I've noticed this with the best turkey
hunters and callers I've known. They possess a kind of quiet confidence.
Sometimes hunters boast, taking complete credit for tagging a turkey
(when their guide may have done the scouting homework and even
called that bird in). On the other hand, the humble veteran of the turkey
woods knows that one day he might be fueled by a recent kill after a successful calling session, while another outing might prove otherwise. That
person looks at the big picture. He isn't keeping score. He doesn't get too
high when things go well or too low when they don't.

In the hands of beginners and veterans, a turkey call is a tool full of
potential, and only that. A friction or mouth call allows you to talk to your
wild quarry, but only if you think like the bird you're hunting. Excessive
hunter movement and ill-timed calling, failing to acknowledge the bird's
keen eyesight, and the fact that you are speaking a language can contribute to shutting turkeys down. If the scene is repeated on consecutive
days, gobblers and hens can feel the pressure, for no birds are warier.

Some hunters believe that simply clucking and softly yelping every
fifteen minutes is the only way to go. But sometimes aggressive calling is
in order, especially when it mimics an excited bird approaching your position. Sometimes only a cluck or soft yelp is called for. In truth, turkey calling—whether you do it in spring, fall, or winter—is an interactive tactic.

How do you actually imitate the diverse turkey vocabulary? What
call do you pull from your vest at specific moments during the hunt?

There is no strategy quite as satisfying as calling a bird into range. After all, you've successfully spoken turkey as a second language and fooled a real gobbler or hen into thinking you're one, too. JOHN HAFNER PHOTO

When do you make these vocalizations? Aspects of fall and winter turkey calling follow here, starting with a brief history, from past to present.

TURKEY CALLING HISTORY

Native Americans crafted and utilized calls to lure the wary wild turkey into range. Necessity demanded it, and their early inventiveness perpetuated the existence of this hunting tool in many forms and variations. The modern outdoor industry continues to capitalize on this original ingenuity. While early history's call makers utilized bones, wood, stone, and other useful available items, these days manmade and natural materials are integrated. Some modern throwback purists only use natural items, as a traditional archer might craft his own bow rather than opt for a modern tricked-out compound.

Call making manifestations have been many, but in the end two kinds of turkey calls existed then as they do now: one requires friction, while the other needs air-activation. Nowadays, hunters own broad personal collections of calls. All of them can be featured in the fall and winter turkey hunt.

The first hint at marketing turkey calls as part of outdoor commerce arose in the late nineteenth century. The Henry C. Gibson red cedar box call emerged then, and his structural style was subsequently varied by many call makers, a trend that continues today. His rectangular box, particularly the innovation of attaching the paddle with a hinge screw, provided the prototype.

Calling history reflects other variations such as cedar scratch boxes, cow and goat horn yelpers, slate calls paired with corn-cob-and-wood strikers (my first turkey call), and so on—all of it useful folk art aimed at talking wild turkey. Native American wingbone calls provided models for the Charles Jordan and Tom Turpin yelpers and others, including the continued modern development of the trumpet call among certain nostalgic call makers.

Ingenuity also insisted that a device be developed to allow the hunter to call without using his hands. Advertisements for the earliest marketed mouth diaphragm calls, specifically the H. P. Bridges version from the 1920s, allude to the portability and easy operation of this tool—at least potentially. The same qualities hold true these days.

FRICTION CALLS

These turkey calls require hand movement to create friction. As a result, hunters often use friction calls to locate and initiate a conversation with unseen but vocal birds. Movement chances at spooking wild turkeys in view, and you need those two hands for shooting. Box, push-pull or push-pin calls, and pot-and-peg options are the most common friction calls.

Friction calls require hand movement. As a result, hunters often use them to locate and initiate a conversation with unseen turkeys before switching to a hands-free diaphragm.

Box calls are slender, rectangular wooden boxes with gently arched sounding-board sides. By working the paddle's bottom against the box call's side lips, the entire turkey vocabulary can be made, including gobbles.

Variations are many. They're generally easy to use—a plus for the beginning hunter and veteran alike. Since a wild turkey answering your call can pinpoint the source of your setup with radar-like ability, then move to your exact location, friction calls can be used to draw that bird in before either switching up to the hands-free diaphragm or going silent as the turkey seeks out your calling location.

Box Calls

These calls are basically slender, rectangular wooden boxes with gently arched sounding-board sides. The paddle (or lid) sits on top and is usually attached with a spring-wrapped hinge screw on one end. This lid's length extends to form a front handle, which is held when calling. By working the paddle's bottom against the box call's side lips, the entire turkey vocabulary can be made, including gobbles. Though box calls take up space, most turkey vests have a lengthy pocket to accommodate them. Although box calls require hand movement, you can conceal one behind a knee or in your lap as you call, with your shotgun or bow in reach, waiting for the moment the turkey's head goes behind a tree or some other obstruction.

Box calls should be held firmly but gently, either horizontally in your left hand's palm as you work the lid with your right (southpaws reverse this), or vertically, with the front handle up high and the screw end down low. As with all calls, it pays to practice regularly until you can render realistic turkey talk. Each box offers different qualities. Boat paddles or so-called long boxes do, too. Tune your call before you hunt as well, even during it, with friction-call chalk, though some modern-day models require no chalking at all. Some are even waterproof, an asset on damp autumn and snowy winter days.

Box Call Basics
- To cluck on a box, pop the paddle off the call's lip with short upward strokes.
- To yelp, cradle the box and lightly scrape and stroke the paddle across the lip.
- To cutt, make a dozen or more fast clucks with sharply repeated pops or taps along the lid.
- To cackle, make a few yelps, and then strike the paddle against the call's lip before finishing with yelps.
- To purr, slowly drag the paddle across the lip. Add soft clucks to this purring to blend calls.
- To kee-kee or kee-kee-run, find the sweet spot on the paddle near the screw end, and then make three whistle-like notes against the lid. Add a yelp or two to render the kee-kee-run. Not all models afford this option. Boat paddles often work best.
- To gobble, wrap a rubber band around the paddle to hold it in place, grip the box call without touching the lid and, while holding the handle end up, shake it.

Push-Pull/Push-Pin Calls
Some hunters call these "idiot boxes," an unfair assertion, as these calling tools require a certain finesse to use effectively. If such calls aren't properly tuned or chalked, the results sound seriously deficient. Most operate based on a long wire that controls plunger tension. The plunger works the movable striking surface across the fixed striker to create turkey sounds. Callers can tweak this device if notes aren't quite right. Some hunters run these calls by gently palming them while working the plunger with the index finger of the same hand, as if pulling a shotgun's trigger. I, however, prefer to cradle this call in my left hand, while I pinch the plunger between my right hand's thumb and index finger and softly stroke it up into the box. This latter technique is particularly effective for making sleepy tree calls to roosted autumn turkeys before fly-down time. I also

run this call by positioning the plunger's tip on my knee, and moving the box up and down to make clucks, yelps, cutts, cackles, and purrs. Chalking the striking surface regularly maximizes this tool's potential. Recent models require no chalking and are waterproof. Some styles are even designed to attach to your shotgun's barrel.

Push-Pull/Push-Pin Call Basics
- To cluck, tap or pop the plunger sharply.
- To yelp, move the plunger with smooth strokes. Some callers push it. Some pull it.
- To cutt, make repeated fast clucks by tapping or popping the plunger. Mix in yelps to imitate an excited turkey.
- To cackle, make a few yelps and then add popping clucks before mixing in yelps to finish.
- To purr, slowly push or pull the plunger so that the movable striking surface drags and skips across the fixed striker.

Scratch boxes
These hand-held calls operate on the same principle as a box, but without the attached paddle. By gently holding the scratch box in one hand and the striker in the other, you can issue clucks, yelps, and purrs. Some callers move the striker against a scratch box's lip (like the bigger box call, or boat paddle, it also has two), while others move the scratch box against the striker's chalked wooden surface. The chamber's empty space between the two lips makes the sound. Strikers need occasional chalking, but are otherwise low maintenance and pocket portable.

Scratch Box Basics
- To cluck, pop the striker off a lip.
- To yelp, drag the striker across a lip.
- To purr, slowly scrape the striker across a lip.

Pot-and-Peg Calls
Most are round, with a striking surface, and require the use of a peg (a.k.a. striker). Striking surfaces vary and include slate, glass, and aluminum, among other manmade materials. Pegs range from wood to glass to carbon to plastic. Some old-schoolers even fashion strikers by gluing a turkey's wingbone to an antiquated brass shotgun hull. While manufactured pegs provided with the pot certainly work, you can experiment with a variety of strikers to render a different tone and volume for clucks, yelps, and purrs. Carbon pegs matched with aluminum or glass surfaces will often work on damp or drizzly autumn days when other strikers

won't, though some manufacturers now offer waterproof pot-and-peg calls.

Striking surfaces must be roughed up (or dressed) to call well. Sandpaper, or fine-grit drywall paper, works on glass surfaces, while some callers use Scotch-Brite scour pads on their slates. Small squares of this material can be carried along on hunts for dressing pot-and-peg calls. Maintain the call's surface by gently sanding in one direction—four or five strokes works fine. Striker tips can also be treated with an emery board.

To operate these calls, hold the pot gently and work the peg like a pen. The striker's tip must touch the surface at all times while calling. Many slates are exceptional for making both gobbler and hen yelps, as well as clucks and purrs. Manufacturer directions provided with your friction call offer a starting point, though all hunters have their own particular styles for making turkey talk.

Pot-and-Peg Basics

- To cluck, put the peg's tip on the striking surface, angle it slightly inward with pressure, and pull it toward you. Keep that tip on the pot. Soft clucks can be made with less pressure; for hard clucks, apply more.

Friction calls are kid-friendly, while diaphragms pose challenges but offer hands-free operation. Here the author's daughter Cora runs her daddy's pot-and-peg call.

- To yelp, draw lines or small ovals on the pot's surface. Less pressure makes softer yelps.
- To cutt, make clucks in fast repetitions by keeping the peg's tip on the surface.
- To cackle, mix yelps, then clucks, then yelps.
- To purr, draw a slow line across the pot's surface. Make these lines in an agitated way to imitate fighting birds, while also adding clucks and cutts at the end of those purrs. Turkeys are often drawn to these inner-flock squabbles.
- To kee-kee, stroke the peg's tip on the striking surface just inside the call's outside rim to create the three-note sound of a young turkey. Add a yelp or two at the end to make the kee-kee-run. Glass surfaces often work best.

AIR-ACTIVATED CALLS

Mouth diaphragms allow hunters to call without hand movements, which are required for friction calls. Such air-activated devices are both inexpensive and easy to carry. Diaphragms are indeed versatile, though such calls are sometimes difficult for beginners to master. Even veterans have occasional trouble.

Pot-and-pegs. Striking surfaces vary, and include slate, glass, and aluminum, among other manmade materials. To operate these calls, you hold the pot gently, and work the peg (a.k.a. striker) like a pen. The striker's tip should touch the surface at all times while calling.

While it's true that a child could pick up a friction call and render acceptable clucks and yelps almost immediately, air-activated calls—which produce turkey sounds by air vibrations—provide a challenge. As diaphragms go, some hunters can handle this foreign object in the roof of their mouth, while others have to fight down the gagging reflex. Manufactured diaphragm options these days include single, double, triple, notched, split, and stacked reeds. Some hunters even make their own calls, or simply call with their natural voice. Other air-activated devices include tube calls, gobbler calls, wing bones, and trumpet calls. Choices are many. In the end, though, you still need to think and act like a turkey to talk like one. Even that kid making the friction call turkey sounds might be puzzled at when to use them.

Mouth Diaphragms

In short, these calls are made by stretching latex rubber across a horse-shoe-shaped frame centered inside a plastic skirt. The caller blows air across the latex reed or reeds to produce turkey sounds. They're so portable you can carry one inside your mouth. They're so affordable you don't really need to worry about losing one. They're so effective, you can continue using lucky diaphragms until tooth marks fray the plastic skirt and the reeds go limp. I always have trouble throwing them away.

While some might argue that a single-reed mouth call should be used by beginners, others feel the double-reed diaphragm is the easiest to handle, especially for making the kee-kee and kee-kee-run of young fall turkeys. As with turkey loads, it's best to try many before you settle on the perfect fit. The best personal diaphragm should allow you to seal that preferred call tight against the roof of your mouth. A firm fit will promote your ability to use this call.

As problems go, the aforementioned gagging reflex typically occurs when the mouth call fits poorly. Trimming the skirt on most calls—sides first, and then the back—can help. Take your time, and don't cut off too much material. Depending on the caller, some mouth calls don't need to be trimmed at all. Smaller diaphragms are also available on the market to fit smaller palates, while others contain a built-in chamber that requires less air pressure to blow.

Assuming you've overcome the previous challenges, it's time to practice. Depending on your family's tolerance, you can do it indoors, settling for the acoustics of a bathroom, basement, or if banished elsewhere, even a pickup truck setting. Listen to tapes of wild turkey vocalizations. By tape recording your mouth calling, you can also work on improving your abilities to match these sounds. Call both indoors and outdoors to hear yourself. Real turkeys in live situations are the best teachers of all. Hunt. A lot.

During the season and as it comes to a close, keep your mouth calls in good working order. Mouth call care should begin as soon as the call comes out of the package. It should be washed with warm water to remove any latex residue. Then, if you prefer, soak it in a solution of one-part mouthwash, one-part water for a few hours before rinsing again. Pat dry, then store your mouth calls in a plastic case or bag in the refrigerator. This provides a cool, dark environment, which keeps reeds tight, providing optimum sound. Diaphragm latex can expand, lose pliability, and create too much vibration if not properly stored.

A flat-tipped toothpick, gently run between the reeds to clean them, helps maintain quality. Be careful not to tear the latex during this process. When storing, place the tip of a toothpick between the reeds so they won't stick together.

In the end, mouth diaphragms free our hands to aim that shotgun or bow when the moment of truth arrives, and with a wary wild turkey, you need all the help you can get.

Diaphragm Call Basics

- To cluck on a mouth diaphragm, say "pock" or "puck" with snapping, beak-like lips (I'm serious—if you've watched a turkey calling when afield, you know exactly what I mean . . . do it when you yelp as well). Pop and smack your lips to make this one- to three-note sound.
- To yelp, your tongue should work the diaphragm into the roof of your mouth, latex edge facing forward, creating an air seal. Next, put your tongue lightly against the latex. Then, blow short yelp-like notes of air, pronouncing the words "chop," "chirp," "chalk," or "chick." Some hunters even say "chee-uck" to create the two-note yelp. Many callers drop their jaws during this action. First, make the high end of the yelp. Roll that note into the lower, deeper part of the yelp by letting tongue pressure off the reed. Break the word you are blowing in half. Say "chee," then "uck." Do it slowly at first, then blend it together. You can break the words chop (ch-op), chirp (ch-irp), chalk (ch-alk), and chick (ch-ick) in half, too, as you yelp with the diaphragm. If you are comfortable with a particular mouth call in the spring, it'll suit you fine in the fall and winter for making lost hen yelps and so forth. Experiment with a variety of diaphragms (and sounds) until you find a style and design you prefer.
- To cutt, run clucks together in a fast series, varying the air you blow across the reeds while also snapping your lips.

- To cackle, make a rapid "kit-kit-kit-cat-cat-cow" call. This call is a series of fast, excited turkey sounds strung together. It imitates a bird flying off the morning roost, and can pull a turkey in at that time.
- To purr, make a fluttering sound with your throat or tongue, as you expel air across the reeds. This call is made in the wild to space feeding turkeys over a food source, and also to indicate a sense of well being, situation depending. An agitated purr can also be tagged on the end of a combination of turkey sounds to imitate fighting birds.
- To kee-kee or kee-kee-run, put a little more tongue pressure on the reed or reeds to get the high note, and then keep the sound rising with a kind of lost urgency. Mimic what you're hearing from young birds. To kee-kee, say "pee-pee-pee," and add a couple yelps after that ("chalk-chalk") for the kee-kee-run. In my experience, double-reed mouth calls work best for imitating young turkeys. Putting more pressure on the reed makes a higher pitch.

Tube Calls

These small tubes are usually fitted with latex single or double reeds like those on a mouth diaphragm. Early calling history reflects examples

Tube calls can be a great fall locator. This simple tool provides yelps and even gobbles by blowing air past the latex and through the tube.

made from snuff boxes. Homemade versions can be crafted from a plastic 35mm film canister. Remove the bottom with a knife, and then stretch a cut strip of medical-glove latex across the open-ended top on the other end. Cut the lid into an open half-moon, and snap it in place over the latex. There should be a thin opening between the remaining uncut lid and the latex edge. Keep that latex tight, and tune routinely.

Tube Call Basics: Once mastered, tube call yelping can be a great fall locator on calm, windless days. This simple call provides loud yelping or rowdy gobbling volume if needed, but also offers soft in-close calling with clucks. Blowing air past the latex, and through the tube makes turkey sounds. Cup your hand or hands around the other end of the call to deaden or project the sound. Manufactured calls vary, so practice is key. Calling instructions are often detailed and helpful with each specific industry option. As with cooking wild game recipes, though, applying advice often involves following basic steps while also free-styling a little. Chances are if you can make the range of turkey calls on a diaphragm, successful tube-call use isn't far behind. However, you may encounter a tickling sensation on your lip when tube calling, or even possess a latex allergy, which like the diaphragm gagging reflex, may push you in the direction of other call choices.

Gobble Calls

These air-activated turkey calls contain three sections: the barrel, sounding chamber, and weighted bellow. These parts create a singular call: the male turkey's gobble. Gobbler calls can be used just before or after morning fly-down, or when a male-only gang of birds is regrouping after a flock bust. Gobbles can be tagged on the end of a kee-kee-run, as fall jakes will often do that. This option is good to have in your autumn and winter calling arsenal. As with all calling in the either-sex-legal turkey woods, these tools should be used with caution.

As a guest at an Alabama turkey camp one year, I had a spirited discussion with some of the locals who insisted male turkeys don't gobble in the fall and winter. Based on some of my spring hunts there, they don't always gobble then, either. Trust that in my longtime experience, male turkeys do gobble in fall and winter (though not necessarily as frequently as in spring). Still it's best to get out there yourself to confirm it.

Gobble Call Basics: Emphasis here is on how you hold this call. To use just one hand, grip the barrel as if throwing a forkball in a baseball game, with your index and middle finger wrapped around it, and your thumb holding the call in place. Swing your wrist forward and back to produce gobbling. Another option is to simply grip the barrel as if holding a glass of water. Swing the call back and forth as if shaking dice. You can also simply pump the call quickly—holding the barrel in one hand and working the weighted bellow up and down in a clean motion with the other. In a common autumn scenario involving young male turkeys, you make a kee-kee-run with a diaphragm before throwing in a gobble at the end.

Wingbone and Trumpet Calls

These calls make up in traditional feeling what they lack in versatility. You can cluck with them. You can yelp with them. The best callers I've met can also kee-kee and kee-kee-run with them. As with the tube call, it can locate a silent bird, which is sometimes all you need. For some, calling in a wild turkey with a tool crafted from the radius and ulna bones of a hen or gobbler they've taken is hard to beat as purist hunting goes. It connects them with calling history—both personal and traditional. It's simple and basic in an age of excessive complexity. Modern callmakers have also adapted some of the original trumpet-call prototypes with their own versions. Others continue to make calls from the wing bones of turkeys they've taken, preferring these to any store-bought options. Such wind instruments can be effective in autumn and winter. Remember, that's what the Native Americans used as a subsistence tool.

Wingbone and Trumpet Call Basics: Practice on wingbone or trumpet calls regularly to make the smack-sucking lip motions necessary to imitate the wild turkey. Gently suck air through the call as you hold its far end cupped in your hands. Smacking, sucking, and drawing air past your pursed lips can alternately make turkey sounds. The trick is in controlling your mouth and throat as you make the proper tone and cadence of clucks and yelps.

Sometimes, I like to mix it up. In an effort to imitate one or more turkeys, I'll yelp on a diaphragm while simultaneously running a friction call. I'll finish one series of kee-kee-runs while continuing with purrs and cutting. I'll empty my vest and put on a calling clinic. It's fun when the action is slow and you need to get something going. At times, it even works. Experiment and try to imagine how you sound to other turkeys nearby. Often that's all it takes to draw birds in for a look-see. If you want to be a whole flock, run a bunch of those calls.

Turkey calling contests judged by human ears are one thing. Vocalizations regarded by real turkeys in a hunting situation are yet another. True enough, many of the top callers have earned their reputations both on the convention stage and in the turkey woods. Then again, just because you'll never chance at hoisting a trophy at such an event doesn't mean you can't

The real contest is between you and the turkey you're calling. Period.
JOHN HAFNER PHOTO

acquire the ability to talk turkey in the woods—and shoulder the ultimate prize. Even some real hens and gobblers would fail to make the first-round cut in a calling contest.

NO-TALK TURKEYS

Let's face it: turkey calls are fun to use, but at times the birds are quiet. They may rely simply on visual evidence that turkeys in their flock are nearby, and that's enough. Other times we may call to a once-vocal bird, only to have it go silent. It may be coming. It may be drifting off. Turkeys are fairly gregarious, but that doesn't always mean they want to investigate your calling.

Yes, it's true that sometimes lost or solitary turkeys will match you call for call, and then come into your setup as if on a long leash. That's gratifying stuff, for sure. Other times too they may show up by walking in silently. Again, patience is key. They're coming to your calls, just not on your watch. To call birds in consistently, you need to maintain a level of confidence. You need to use all the available calls at times, or just a few favorites. You need to fight the urge to fidget while waiting on birds. To

Cold calling, not to be confused with calling when it's cold, is an effort to evoke responses from silent turkeys.

learn this, you may need to experience the awful feeling of standing up, perhaps persecuted by early fall's biting bugs or late autumn's chill, only to have a silent wild turkey flush nearby. You didn't hear it, so you thought it wasn't there. Yes you called that bird in. Yes the game might be over—for now. Yes you might be able to locate that turkey once more, and call it back if you reposition. Maybe other flock members are regrouping, too, so just sit tight. Relax. Trust yourself. If there's fresh sign of turkeys, hang in there.

And when that turkey answers your call, then hunts down that sound you're making in the fall or winter woods—completely fooled that your bird talk is real—and you punctuate that fine moment with a single killing shot, you'll be glad you're alive. Turkey calls are tools with a fine historical tradition, and yes, I've kissed a call or two in those giddy post-game moments.

FALL AND WINTER LOCATOR CALLING

It was one of those *Silence of the Gobs* situations, a private viewing for this fall turkey hunter. Though I'd located and called up autumn longbeards before, I was dealing with a brood hen, and its early-hatch flock on this hunt.

I knew they were somewhere close by. The group of birds had been feeding in a farmer's field the previous late afternoon. I'd glassed them there, noting where they might roost nearby. Here I was the next morning, well before dawn, waiting on sunrise. Problem is, they stayed quiet as light filtered into the woods.

Fingering my striker, I plucked a soft cluck off the slate face. Not fifty steps away, a bird answered back. Bingo. I settled in, shotgun balanced on my knee. That was it for several long minutes. I issued a cluck, then several soft yelps, and that same turkey mimicked me.

After a period of waiting, several turkeys began flying down and calling to each other. Rooted there on my butt, I couldn't move. Efforts to call them in were ignored for lack of visual evidence: they saw no live turkey near my setup. And so the flock moved off. I'd have to locate them again.

By midmorning, I'd slowly moved along a likely path of travel between their roost and feeding source—the farmer's field. I offered a lost yelp. A turkey in the field answered. Game on, again. Slipping into position on the pasture edge, I called, and that turkey responded, moving closer.

Soon, I saw the lead bird, the brood hen—vocal and insistent—pulling a cluster of family-flock turkeys toward my position. I offered a kee-kee-run with my mouth call, and a fall jake answered in same, and then threw in a squawky-gobble. The juvenile gobbler eventually broke off from the group, came in, and I dropped him.

Twice these autumn birds had been silent, and twice I'd located them by cold calling. Locator calling for wild turkeys, spring, fall, or winter, requires two simple basics: you make a sound, then listen for a bird's response, revealing its position. In spring, we traditionally imitate a barred owl, crow, or some other loud call to get a spring tom to shock gobble, often on its roost. In fall, however, this strategy is unlikely to get a response.

Cold calling to locate wild turkeys is another two-season option. You can cluck, yelp, and even gobble to find once-silent spring toms. This can also be done to evoke responses from autumn and winter turkeys. Though underutilized, cold calling to legal but shut-mouthed either-sex birds improves your ability to find fall and winter turkeys. During the woodstove months, you'll attempt to locate family flocks, broodless hen groups, and gobbler gangs.

If you know male turkeys have roosted nearby and flown down, make gobbler yelps, fighting purrs, gobbles, and kee-kee-runs to get birds like this pair to answer. They might come right in for a look. JOHN HAFNER PHOTO

Since roosted autumn and winter turkey flocks involve adult groups or family flocks with brood hens and juvenile birds of either sex, the calling you make and encounter before fly-down will differ.

Tree calling involves three primary turkey vocalizations: clucking, yelping, and gobbling. Used to encourage silent tree-bound turkeys to sound off, cold calling can be varied to reveal flock members' exact or probable location.

Roost Clucking (Either Sex)
One tree-bound cluck made by turkeys indicates contentment, while the other—often called "pitting" or "putting"—is an urgent alarm call. The first is a sound made by roosted birds before fly-down to ask, "Where are you? I'm here." The other, the pitting cluck, says, "Predator below. Get ready to flush." You hear it on getting too close to roosted birds.

Hunting Situation: Turkeys are roosted. You want them to fly down nearby, and come to your calls.

Hunter's Locator Call: Set up where you've roosted fall turkeys or expect flocks might sleep. Make this plain cluck with one to three soft notes. Space this effort out. Avoid clucking loudly, at least at first. Less is more when trying to locate turkeys just waking up in the morning.

Ground Clucking (Either Sex)
The plain cluck is one to three spaced notes.

Hunting Situation: Turkeys have flown down, assembled, and moved off. You want to find them.

Hunter's Locator Call: Leave several seconds between your clucks when trying to locate unseen birds. Clucks and alarm putts are similar. Both attempt to get another turkey's attention. Cutting, as it's typically called, is simply a series of loud clucks with an irregular, urgent rhythm, and the same pitch. This can also be used to evoke a response from a silent single bird or flock member.

Roost Yelping (Hens)
Soft, nasal yelping often begins in the false dawn, or as daylight breaks. Its purpose is to notify flock members of their specific locations before fly-down. Often a brood hen makes this sound in autumn situations. Broodless hen groups will communicate this way before fly-down, too.

Hunting Situation: Roosted turkeys are waking up and getting ready to fly down. Your soft yelping to birds on the roost might pull the flock into range when they hit the ground. You are trying to act like one of those turkeys.

Hunter's Locator Call: Cold calling with soft yelps can be made in a location where you've found fresh turkey tracks, scratchings, droppings, or feathers. You need to be close to the roost to hear responses to your locator yelping. Once you cold call with soft hen yelps, listen intently for a turkey to call back to your vocalizations. Don't overdo it, though, as this call is muted, generally three to five notes long.

Ground Yelping (Hens)
A plain yelp has roughly three to nine notes, and is made with less urgency than an assembly or lost yelp. An assembly yelp is made by the brood hen to gather young turkeys after fly-down, or following a flock break. When separated, a lost yelp is made by individual adult hen turkeys (or sub-two-year-old hens in their second fall) to indicate they are looking for other birds. Both assembly and lost yelping have more notes (15 or 20 isn't unusual) and are louder and often raspier than the typical plain yelp. A hen's yelping is also generally higher pitched than a gobbler's.

Hunting Situation: Make the plain or lost yelp to locate adult or juvenile turkeys while cold calling in the fall.

Hunter's Locator Call: Lost yelping is one way to pull a response from nearby but silent birds. Kee-keeing and kee-kee-running is another, as it will sometimes evoke an assembly call from the brood hen, which, like the lost yelp, is urgent and many-noted.

Roost Yelping (Gobblers)
Fall jakes and so-called super jakes born in the spring or summer of the previous year sometimes offer raspy, slower two- to three-note yelps on the roost. Juvenile gobblers born that year add a gobble on such calling as well—occasionally a poor barking effort at best. As with roosted hen yelping, these vocalizations are soft and muted.

Hunting Situation: Roost yelping can be used to locate silent male birds on the roost and to evoke responses from these turkeys, revealing their position.

Hunter's Locator Call: Set up near a likely roost site, near where you've noted gobblers the afternoon before, and call as first light arrives.

Ground Yelping (Gobblers)
Once on the ground, gobbler yelping can be louder and more intense. As with roost yelping, it includes several notes.

Hunting Situation: You know gobblers have roosted nearby, flown down, and you want to find them. Gobbler yelp to get a bird to answer.

Another scenario might include evoking a response from a gobbler group you've flushed. Often your initial call will get others talking back.

Hunter's Locator Call: Slate calls are superb at creating raspy gobbler yelps. Many mouth calls available tend to be higher-pitched to imitate hens. If you have a diaphragm that is low-pitched, use it to make gobbler yelps as well.

Roost Gobbling

While some hunters might argue gobblers don't gobble at all outside of spring, experience shows otherwise. Outside the breeding season, male birds continue to focus on establishing, contesting, and maintaining pecking-order status. They gobble on the autumn roost not to attract hens, but to vocalize their presence to other male birds.

Hunting Situation: You know where gobblers might roost, and you want to pin that location down.

Hunter's Locator Call: Use a gobbler call at daybreak to elicit a response from roosted male turkeys, allowing you to note their position.

Ground Gobbling

Fall gobblers gobble to each other. Adult longbeards do it after fly-down and to regroup in post-flush situations.

Hunting Situation: You want to raise a response from a male bird in the woods or locate the presence of a gobbler after a flushing situation.

Hunter's Locator Call: Gobble to adult toms in a cold-calling situation or during a post-flush, call-back session. Add a gobbler call on the end of a kee-kee-run to locate juvenile males.

STARTING A FIGHT

Interested in making silent fall and winter gobblers more vocal? If you've roosted male turkeys that are staying quiet on their limbs, set up nearby before daybreak, then start a fight after fly-down. If you've ever heard a group of male birds in a post-roost rumble, you know that the event is rowdy and loud.

To evoke this kind of response so that gobblers might come running to your setup, start out with muted clucking and gobbler yelping while turkeys are still roosted.

When you have a sense that fly-down time is nearing, use your hat or another manufactured device to imitate the wing beats of turkeys clawing through tree branches. This is optional, but some hunters do it.

After this, make your gobbler yelping more agitated and your calling more insistent. Using both a mouth call for yelping (avoid high-pitched diaphragms) and a slate call to make urgent yelping and fighting purrs, you can sometimes draw a gang of male birds in for a look.

Add gobbles to the calling clinic you're offering as well, but always with safety in mind. You can also use that hat or wing beat-making device to imitate gobblers hitting each other as they purr.

At any rate, this kind of extreme fall calling should be made only once or twice during the fly-down period as birds move off the roost to the ground. Prolonging it is unrealistic.

You can also use this fighting approach if you're just entering a pure situation during a hunt, and some time has passed between fly-down and turkeys are walking about on the ground. Often gobblers will sound off as they approach. In such situations, I've seen autumn longbeards strut and gobble with anticipation as they draw nearer.

CHAPTER 7

Edge cover and uncut grass holds bugs, and turkeys gravitate there. September and October flocks can be in the margins separating woods and pastures. If grasshoppers haven't been frosted off, turkeys will feed on these and other field bugs.

JOHN HAFNER PHOTO

Fall and Winter Roosts

Wild turkeys sleep in trees. You can slip close to roost sites early—at least within earshot—while they still grip branches with their long toes and scaly feet and begin your morning's hunt there.

One gray October dawn in New York state, seated on an elevated spine of woods at the base of big oak, soft tree-calling turkey talk to the east confirmed I'd nailed down the flock's roost. Great. My timeworn slate and rosewood striker mimicked a response, which was sleepily echoed by several birds. Silence followed. I put the friction call down on the ground next to me, and waited, a double-reed diaphragm seated in the roof of my mouth.

Some time later, a handful of dark forms flew down, assessed their ground-standing situation, and slowly began mincing steps toward my position. Subtle turkey talk filled the autumn woods. I softly called: kee-kee-kee-yawp. A fall jake broke off from the group, offered a kee-kee-run, then gobbled. I stifled the smile under my facemask. The morning's hunt looked good. If anything, I wanted it to last a little, but such opportunities come and go just as fast.

You guessed it. Less than a minute later, I had that lanky bird by the feet, grateful for the moment. As if scripted, the sky began to spit snow, and the rising wind (an enemy to all turkey hunters who value listening to, and calling birds) picked up. Talk about relief. Is it always this easy? Heck no, but identifying where to start your hunting day surely helps.

WHY WE ROOST BIRDS
Roost is a noun, a place where turkeys spend the night. Roost is also a verb, an active effort to find where turkeys sleep. The wild turkey's sharp eyesight, superb hearing, and instinctive wariness make it necessary to

A fall jake broke off from the group, offered a kee-kee-run, then gobbled. I stifled the smile under my facemask. The morning's hunt looked good. JOHN HAFNER PHOTO

determine where individual birds or flocks rest at night in order to hunt them effectively the next day—after they fly down out of those trees. Finding where they gather among tree limbs gives you the obvious advantage of starting the day with the turkeys nearby. While flocks seem to have an uncanny ability to assemble together after fly-down, only to move off away from your seated position, every so often it all comes together and you can be among those turkeys as they regroup in the morning—ideally in gun or bow range. If you want, setting up there when they return to roost at night can also help you tag a bird—or at least to get close to them and roost them for the next morning.

Roosting time is often a half-hour to fifteen minutes before true dusk. Some roosting areas might be used annually, so study them regularly. Sometimes a flock may have several different areas it favors, often depending on nearby food sources, which can vary seasonally.

Slip into such turkey-holding locations undetected, ideally an hour or more before fly-up, and sit down on your portable cushion, fully camouflaged. Watch. Wait. Don't move too much. Relax. Take a nap if need be. A half-hour before official sunset, listen attentively from your position. You may be able to hear squirrels and crows pestering flocks. You may see birds fly up while you scan the nearby woods. Turkeys clawing and winging up through branches make a welcomed and unmistakable racket as they elevate into treetops. You may hear soft clucks once birds are in trees. Depending on your hearing ability, on a calm late afternoon you might note birds a quarter-mile away, especially if they're calling. On stormy evenings, it might be considerably tougher.

Once you've confirmed that turkeys are indeed winging up into a particular section of the woods, wait for darkness to fall, then slip out of there quietly. A small penlight can help you negotiate darkened terrain. If you are scouting potential roosting sites with a buddy or two, take listening and viewing positions spread out along that location. Later, on the drive back to turkey camp, you can compare notes. Often in such cases, one person may not have heard a thing, while another might have the flock's position nailed down.

Roosting fall and winter birds the night before you pursue them is best. Sometimes you don't need to be right out there sitting with the turkeys. You can also glass hunting and roosting locations with binoculars from a road in late afternoon. Usually a flock that has been feeding in fields will then make its steady procession toward the nearby woods as darkness approaches. Chances are they won't be far away the next morning. From your vehicle, you may even note likely roosting areas without absolute confirmation. If there's a spot with big-branched trees and concealing cover nearby, that's where they'll probably spend time at night. They may even sleep above water.

WATER ROOSTS

Wild turkeys around the United States sometimes choose roosting trees that put them above water. From Pennsylvania to Virginia, and Missouri to Maine, I've seen Eastern wild turkeys favor sleeping locations above beaver ponds, mountain brooks, pasture watering holes, and river sloughs. I've seen these birds choose big trees in flooded timber many times, often flying a football field from dry land to get there.

In Florida, Osceola turkeys often choose to sleep in cypress swamps, flying down to sandy gray-white farm roads or trails, feeding in open pastures, and loafing in oak hammocks. In Texas, Rio Grande flocks may also put themselves above water, if available—then again, I've even seen them roost in dense live oaks above dry creek beds, too. Rios are routinely challenged to find good places to roost, and even manmade structures might do.

Out West, river systems with nearby roosting trees often hold Merriam's turkeys as well. Find ponderosa pines nearby? How about cottonwoods? Check out those areas as possible roosts. By day flocks can roam widely. By night they sleep in such places, location depending.

Keep in mind that turkeys feel less threatened when sleeping in trees above the ground and choosing branches that also hang above water. If I'm in a new hunting situation, I invariably gravitate toward the nearest available water source in my effort to scout for roosting locations. If anything, tracks are easier to detect there. It doesn't always hold true, but many times it does.

Suffice it to say it's tough to listen for turkeys flying up into trees if the mountain stream over which they roost is noisily making its way downhill. In such situations, you may have to make visual confirmation.

If turkeys are roosted in the limbs of water-rooted trees above beaver ponds and lake shallows, your chances at identifying droppings are nearly nil. Unless your hearing is sharp enough and time spent there is long enough to hear the occasional plop of droppings falling from above, you'll need direct visual or auditory confirmation.

For flocks that rest by night in wooded or open locations away from water, turkey leavings will be prominent. Abundant, piled, fresh droppings below likely roosting trees almost always confirm a recent roost. A mix of old and new droppings assures it. You can check out these spots while the turkeys are somewhere else during the day. Again, they will also roost above dry creek beds, which will be loaded with droppings and other sign.

FOOD SOURCES AND ROOSTS

Find the food, and the roost may be nearby. If fresh droppings, feathers, tracks, and other turkey sign are near a favored food source late in the day, the roosting cover is probably not far away. Often in the fall and winter, turkeys will not only roost in an area that provides a sense of security, but also in a direct path to the field or woods where they eat each morning and late afternoon. In early fall, flocks often favor insects. Edge cover holding uncut grass contains bugs, and turkeys gravitate there. September and October flocks can be in the margins separating woods and pastures. If grasshoppers haven't been frosted off, turkeys will hit these and other field bugs. Once the post-freeze transition takes place, if mast is around, wild turkeys will search for beechnuts, acorns, fruits, and tubers, among other available edibles.

Human intervention in agricultural areas, especially in late afternoon, can move wild turkeys from one favored nighttime roost to another. Not everyone is hunting fall wild turkeys like you, and if a farmer happens to be in his field with a tractor late in the day, or if ATVs have moved through the nearby area on that occasion, flocks may change their routine and sleep somewhere else. Recreational outdoor users are varied. Crop fields get attention. Turkeys take notice.

Field setups in agricultural areas allow you to watch roosted turkeys fly directly into open spaces where they feed.

Later on, after northern frosts, turkeys may spend more time in the woods eating hard and soft mast (nuts or fruits used as wildlife food sources). To find roosts, determine what turkeys are eating, and where they are doing it. Again, roosting trees likely aren't far away.

If possible, establish field setups to watch turkeys fly directly into open areas that hold food sources—including field spots in the deep woods. If the fall and winter flock is large, it's quite a sight as they sail down from up on high. If the morning is quiet enough, you can some-times hear the air whistling through their wing feathers.

OOPS, THEY FLUSHED!

Nobody's perfect. At daybreak or dusk, you may stumble into a roosted flock unintentionally. Once the alarm putting begins in the trees above you, all turkeys in listening range are alerted. It's then you should con-sider walking (or running) around the area in an attempt to be seen until birds begin to flush. If you happen into birds at dusk, flush them on your way out, then return in the morning. If you happen to bump them at day-break, scatter the turkeys by walking beneath them, then hunt from that flush site as they regroup. Just because you didn't know they were there doesn't mean you can't capitalize on your unexpected find.

Roosted fall and winter turkeys can make quite a racket. To locate roosts by listening, be there early enough to slip into the woods undetected. Loud yelping, cackling, gobbling, and other turkey sounds will often be heard as daybreak approaches, then right after fly-down. Your window of listening time might be short after that, as flocks can go from rowdy to absolutely silent once they hit the ground. I swear sometimes they vaporize.

At dawn, a single contented cluck, or agitated roosting "pit" sound in a tree might mean you're close to a roosting area (or just near a solitary bird). You might be on the edge of it, or right in the middle. Freeze in place. Sit down, calls ready. You may not need to frantically flush them if only detected by one bird. The silence that might follow it may leave you puzzled, though. Be patient. As mentioned, the clawing of feathers through trees and the ticking of wingtips brushing tree branches at fly-down time can key you into turkeys without them ever making another peep.

Focused listening can even help you count general bird numbers in a flock without seeing them and also distinguish flock composition once they start calling after they hit the ground. It's okay to set up close to the roosted birds (especially in the pre-dawn dark before game time); especially if you know they're there. Listening intently helps. Like morning fly-down sounds, fly-up noises of turkeys going to roost can put you where you need to be.

ROOSTING BY SUBSPECIES

As mentioned, Eastern wild turkeys sometimes favor roosts over rivers, streams, or swamps. Pines are often chosen for concealing cover, as are big hardwood stands. In upland habitats, turkeys might prefer sloping roosts on ridges. Hemlocks. White pines. Oaks. Eastern wild turkeys sleep in all three. During storms, flocks may seek shelter elsewhere.

Merriam's flocks sometimes roost in conifer stands where available, often favoring these spots through successive broods since such cover is sometimes marginal. Location depending, other roost sites might include Douglas firs, white firs, ponderosa pines, or southwestern white pines.

Florida turkeys favor tree roosts in cypress swamps, with oaks and piney woods providing habitat. Available roosting cover in their native Osceola range will be found near an available food source. Invariably, water will be nearby, or even beneath, roosts.

Rio Grande turkeys make the best of available roosting habitat, often selecting the tallest trees or even brushy cover. This can include live oak,

Fall and winter turkeys often stay in the sheltering cover of trees during snowy periods. JOHN HAFNER PHOTO

cottonwood, willow, hackberry, and the pecan tree species, often near a permanent water source throughout their range. Rios aren't adverse to manmade roosting structures. Power line supports, oil tanks, and windmill towers can all hold birds.

Gould's turkeys roost in the Mexican Chihuahua and Apache pines, cottonwoods, and oaks. In southern New Mexico, Gould's flocks routinely roost in the same locations nightly due to limited options.

In rainy and snowy weather, turkeys may linger on the roost well after the assumed fly-down time. During periods of heavy snow, they may never leave the sheltering cover of trees. On windy days, they may roost in an out-of-the-way ravine or draw. On a clear, starry fall night, turkeys might choose to roost up high. On stormy days, down low. A quiet, windless morning is best for locating roosts, but hey, if you want to hunt, you have to be out there—calm days or not.

Get as close as you can, within reason. You can of course get out there in the dark and wait for daybreak to arrive. Setting up at the base of a tree in which a turkey sleeps, or facing one on the roost, is indeed possible using the extreme get-in-there-early approach. Once installed, though, you can't move as daylight comes, as you can be easily detected. Ideally, you should set up some distance away to watch the whole scene unfold at fly-down time. Extreme roosting setups can involve a portable pop-up blind. Using this option, you can be close and undetected—assuming the birds don't simply fly down the other way. With blinds, mobility is always limited.

A FEW OF MY FAVORITE ROOSTS

There's one roost in New York State that holds turkeys year-round. It's a steep hillside, with hardwoods towering tall above it. A small creek trickles far below those treetops. Once roosted, turkeys have many fly-down options. Near the top, they can scan a flat hilltop shelf and wing down there. They can sail down to a cornfield far below or simply hop down into the woods if they wish and begin the day. For the most part, they have the advantage of elevation and landing options.

There are several similar roosting spots where I bowhunt in New Hampshire that seem to hold birds every fall—gobblers, family flocks, you name it. These locations aren't much to look at: just big bull pines, with their requisite broad branches for roosting, set off from hardwoods but adjacent to swamps. The areas beneath those big trees are routinely used as dusting areas, as the loose, pine-needle-covered soil allows it. All are elevated, bench-like in appearance, above the swampy bottoms but near small game trails that lead to open crop fields. (Those trails are always tattooed with deer tracks as well.) Turkeys like such surroundings.

The author took this opening day New York fall turkey by setting up close to the roost, then calling the bird in at sunrise after fly-down.

There's one in Vermont situated above a small stream with gurgling plunge pools. That water flows off a side hill, and the towering oaks and maples along its snaking presence hold turkeys. I'm so confident in it that I can leave in the middle of the night, drive three hours, and arrive in the pre-dawn dark, knowing that a quiet walk up the hill will likely put me near birds. Once, after a slow walk in, I sat down in the dark and witnessed daybreak present a magnificent longbeard on a limb right in front of me. "Roosted ain't roasted," the saying goes. How that tom got away I'll never know.

In Texas, landowners often insist that hunters avoid putting pressure on roost-challenged Rio Grande flocks, preferring that birds be permitted to fly down and regroup before you move on them. In Florida, snakes, gators, and swamp water sometimes make Osceola turkey roosts tough to approach directly. Merriam's flocks might roost where you find them—not actually officially migratory, but somehow just a little restless too as fall shifts to winter.

Once you find that favorite roost, the information is special. Share it with friends, or develop amnesia, it's your personal call.

UP THEY GO

I've watched turkeys calmly ease into a wooded area, then fly-hop a short distance up into the tree they want to sleep in. Sometimes they'll use branches to step their way up. Other times, they may choose a high knob on a field top, then walk-run down a slope before taking off like a jetliner, sailing a long ways before landing on a branch. Occasionally flock members may not fly to roost at the same time. Once in the trees, they may change limbs and make plenty of noise doing so. Sometimes it's clear to me that turkeys I've roosted in one spot move to another location—often not too far away—during the night.

Call me crazy, but it's clear that some movement goes on after dark. I've certainly seen this repositioning of roosted birds in the dim light just after dusk. I've heard that some transplanted Rio Grande turkeys in Hawaii even roost on the ground since no predators challenge their numbers. At any rate, you may witness preening, hear sticks falling, and note soft calling by roosting turkeys. Only once can I remember a turkey flying back down after it had roosted. Maybe it was eager to start the next day.

At roosting time, turkeys will often ease toward a wooded area, look around, and then fly into the tree they want to sleep in. Be there the next morning.
JOHN HAFNER PHOTO

By noting flock composition, you can determine whether or not taking an either-sex juvenile hen or gobbler— legal in most autumn and winter hunting states—can be part of your game plan.

JOHN HAFNER PHOTO

Changing Flock Composition

While there's a saying in October turkey camp that goes: "In spring we hunt gobblers, but in fall we hunt turkeys," identifying flock composition based on gender—even during legal either-sex hunts—presents options before, during, and after time afield.

Once, while pursuing autumn hens and gobblers in New York State's Catskills region, I noted fresh hillside scratchings. I had road-tripped there too late to hunt them off their morning roost. The exposed areas beneath raked leaves where turkeys had recently fed held occasional popcorn-shaped droppings often attributed to adult hens, though some would have qualified as gobbler leavings. My English setter Midge, also a bird lover, noted them and the scent left by the turkeys passing through there recently.

Following these fresh scratchings and droppings, we moved south along the sunny hillside and finally located the flock nearly a half-mile from where we'd started. Midge moved ahead, just out of sight at one point. Her sharp yips and barking, plus the frantic wing beats of flushing turkeys and alarm putting, followed. One fishhooked overhead and down the hill. Several flashed darkly against the tall hardwoods, wings gleaming in the afternoon light. A few more ran toward the ridge top. We'd done it.

We'd made game, sure enough, but that's just the start of decoding flock composition. I called to Midge, picked a broad oak's trunk for a backrest, and constructed a quick blind of deadfall and camouflaged burlap I was lugging. I concealed my snow-white dog in a zippered leaf-patterned bag, and settled in. Now came the waiting. The birds seemed big. Adult hens? Super jakes? I thought the former, but I couldn't tell just yet.

Maybe forty-five minutes later, flapping wings said a nearby turkey had flown out of its tree, and crunching leaves said it had started walking up the hill toward our setup near the flush site. Game time. That single turkey clucked and I echoed right back.

I felt that sweet, blood-thumping tension hunters crave as a wild turkey approaches into range. An adult hen's yelp followed. I mimicked it. Midge stirred at the calling, and I hoped she'd settle just long enough for me to get a shot off. Another bird clucked up the hill, then one directly in front of me—far off but on the ground. Surrounded by adult hens, and likely some hens born two springs ago as well—all broodless and running together as a flock—I heard hen yelping, cutting, purring, and clucking, but no urgent calling whatsoever from juvenile wild turkeys. Nor did I hear gobbler yelping. Best I could tell, eight female birds surrounded us. It was so raucous I was sure we'd soon see them all slip into range like a fall turkey hunter's dream.

Not so. I clucked, I yelped, and one hen drew close, but on the other side of a little rise—heard but not seen. I guessed it to be no further than five steps away off my shotgun's muzzle: too close. Rustling footsteps in the leaves up the hill told me other birds had seen this one, and soon they all regrouped, hen yelping and clucking until they got together. Game over: they vaporized into cover as the afternoon waned. A profound and heavy silence followed that only turkey hunters know.

Had it been earlier in the afternoon, I could have released Midge again for a second flock break. As darkness eased in, I resolved to try for them the following day, and with the truck a half-mile away in unfamiliar woods, we set off.

Nope, I didn't kill a legal hen turkey this particular day, nor did I succeed the next morning (a gusty rainstorm blew in, and we never found them again), but such encounters often serve to school hunters in successfully decoding the mysteries of flock composition for other future outings. Once that's done—day-to-day, week-to-week, year-to-year—you can learn how to approach situations based on this understanding. I've had such broodless flock interactions since then. Sometimes I've won. Often they have, but I thoroughly enjoy every memory.

CHANGING FLOCK COMPOSITION

You walk away from every hunt with some tidbit of new information to gnaw on. In the lead example, the way the birds acted on regrouping—making adult hen calls, and not juvenile vocalizations, nor gobbler yelps—told me we'd encountered a broodless group of female turkeys. Hunting a flock composed of the brood hen and her young-of-year charges might have involved a different approach. For one thing, calling would have included kee-kees and kee-kee-runs. A single brood hen would have started her assembly yelp nearby, while I would have countered by trying to kee-kee or kee-kee-run to one of the juvenile birds, hoping to draw a young turkey to my calling first by imitating a flock mate.

By routinely noting flock composition this way, you can determine whether or not taking an either-sex juvenile gobbler or hen—legal in most autumn and winter hunting states—can be part of your game plan.

Seasonal changes dictate that the brood hen rules the family flock through summer, and from early to mid-fall. In late autumn and early winter, unruly juvenile males leave the family unit in woods-roaming short-bearded groups (beards appear at about five months of age, growing roughly five inches annually). After their departure, the brood hen and hens-of-the-year compose these flocks, with leadership restored.

Adult and juvenile gobblers flock together in spring and then summer, after breeding ends, as hens begin to nest and hatch broods. Like the broodless adult hens, male birds will often travel in groups through autumn and into the heart of winter. In spring, these male turkeys will seek out hens, and some will stay together even while doing so.

During the woodstove months and into winter, adult and juvenile wild turkeys of both sexes will sometimes flock up together to create massive, mixed-brood groups within a particular habitat, especially if food sources are limited. Gobbler gangs might also travel to the same general area as family flocks but remain aloof and at a distance. Some wild turkeys travel alone.

To hunt effectively, we need to understand flock composition and then how it changes. Alliances can vary, but some basic flock configurations are regularly identifiable.

Family Flocks

Wild turkeys hatch throughout the spring and summer, depending on when the hen bred and successfully nested. Since hatching times are varied, some autumn family groups contain young birds (especially males) the size of the adult brood hen. Other such fall flocks might have a recognizable female turkey leading birds-of-the-year that is considerably smaller. Biology tells us a typical clutch is eight to twelve eggs. A single-family flock of a dozen birds is large. Predators take their fill.

A brood hen with just a single young bird or just several more can be occasionally seen due to predation or weather factors, while big groups of several juvenile flocks and brood hens can be noted as well. These family flocks stay together until juvenile males leave to form their own jake groups in late fall. As mentioned, later in the autumn season, young gobblers tend to dominate flocks even more than adult hens, creating obvious disharmony. By then, they move on to form jake-only flocks. Sometimes these small male groups meet up with other gobblers in the area, too.

Juvenile Flocks Without Brooding Hens

Fall turkey hunters sometimes wonder whether it's okay to legally take a brood hen from a family flock. I've put this question to biologists, and they generally agree that the flock's survival chances are good, as young birds grow wary over summer and into autumn. They have to. As a prey species, turkeys have it tough on a daily basis—young and adult alike. Late hatch flocks, those with pheasant-sized juveniles as hunting seasons begin likely have more of a challenge, what with less experience in the wild.

This past late summer, through fall and into late winter, I watched a flock of nine juvenile turkeys without a brood hen. They had chosen a roughly five-acre area (split by the busy interstate highway) for their home ground and roosted there. I'd see them on an almost daily basis, hugging the edge cover and silently feeding on available foods. Why they were without a brood hen is anyone's guess (roadkill?), but I watched through the months as the gobblers—four, all told—grew to be easily distinguished from the smaller hens in the flock: red heads, black-tipped breast feathers, and sprouting beards told the story.

All winter they remained, disturbed only briefly by gawking motorists like myself, whereupon they would vanish into thicker, albeit limited, wooded cover. I never once heard any calling from that spot, and assume they got together daily on a purely visual basis. Some days I wouldn't see them at all, just their tracks crossing the snowy on-ramp. Days later they'd be back. At one point in late winter, a young hen turned up dead along the major highway, having wandered out of the tight habitat.

As spring approached, I noted that all four young gobblers were suddenly gone from the group in their wanderlust mode. Not long after, a strutting mature longbeard had moved into the small area, and collected the remaining four hens for his effort. I never heard a gobble from him, either, though I would listen for it at daybreak. Shortly after that, all of the turkeys were gone—all this several weeks before the spring hunting season opened.

Can a family flock survive without their brood hen? In this case, noting the loss of the single young hen, yes. Do turkeys go silent in a

Young late fall and winter gobblers, like this one, begin to dominate family flocks, creating obvious disharmony. By winter they form jake-only groups.

JOHN HAFNER PHOTO

challenging situation when getting together visually makes calling unnecessary? In this case, maybe.

Jake-Only Flocks

Fall jakes born that year become dominant before they leave the family flock in late autumn or winter, challenging the brood hen's status. A single dominant jake will sometimes even call family flock members back together after the morning fly-down or after a predator (or hunter) flushes them. Flock harmony is disrupted for a time. While in the family group, and after they leave it, male turkeys routinely fight to establish pecking order.

In jake-only flocks, a dominant bird usually rules this entire group—until status is contested. This is why some of us have shot a gobbler, only to see other male birds move right in to peck at, claw, and mock breed the dead turkey. The survivors want top-dog status. As fall and winter

In jake-only flocks, a dominant bird usually rules the entire group—status is often contested. JOHN HAFNER PHOTO

progresses, these jakes will often join one or more adult gobblers. One bird in that group—often a longbeard—will hold spring breeding rights to all the hens in the area; that is, unless its position is challenged. Nevertheless, it's also not uncommon to see a band of jakes defeat an adult gobbler in a fight. I've watched gangs of juvenile turkeys run off longbeards, and vice-versa.

Year-and-a-Half Gobblers

Called "jake-and-a-halves" or "super jakes" by us turkey hunters, these male birds are roughly sixteen to eighteen months old when autumn arrives, depending on geographical location. Distinguished from male birds under a year old, their beards are five to eight inches long. Their spurs are still less than an inch. Their tail fans are full. They run together in small groups, often the same birds they spent time with that past spring. They can appear identical, which suggests they were from the same brood. They work well to the autumn hunter's call, often gobbling and even strutting, and provide a lot of enjoyment during the fall hunt. Their weight in your vest's game pocket is substantial.

Remember, this is the same bird you passed on in spring because he had a beard resembling a stubbed-out cigar. Some autumn hunters will kill a super jake and refer to it as a longbeard. That's fine. Technically it is, I guess, but a wild gobbler that's been alive for two years or more is often an entirely different creature.

Adult Longbeards

Spring turkey hunters often prefer to take a dominant adult longbeard. As a result, there are often fewer available in the fall woods for us to hunt. In places like Missouri and Texas, where turkey densities are large, fall longbeards are more common. Other locations see fewer. In fall and winter, sometimes these adult birds run alone, or with super jakes, and/or juvenile males born that past late spring or summer. They may also be solitary.

After the New Hampshire bow season for turkeys ended one mid-December, I noted the single tracks of an adult tom. I watched this gobbler off and on through that snowy winter. He rarely varied his daily pattern, moving from his preferred roosts—different tall, big-branched white pines—to several farmers' fields where the gobbler could find waste corn in spread manure, the so-called "hot lunch program" for Snow Belt turkeys. Spring arrived, then the opening day of the May gobbler season. The longbeard came home with me that morning. Though his range included the several adjoining farms, changing roosting trees occasionally within that general area, he had not varied his day-to-day travels appreciably for roughly six months. I had scouted him that whole time.

While this might be an isolated case, solitary longbeards can be iden-tified this way in fall and winter, assuming your season is open. You can also study them during this time with the spring in mind.

Hen-Only Flocks

Juvenile females, or jennies as some call them, tend to remain with the brood hen until spring. Around then, you'll often see single young or adult hens traveling alone, driven by biology to breed, find nesting loca-tions, and hatch broods. Years ago, on a Florida spring hunt, I was rou-tinely amazed to find myself calling in flocks of a half-dozen or more hens in different locations. Only one time during that particular stormy trip did I yelp up a solitary Osceola longbeard to the gun, and never did I see male birds with females. Weather? Timing? Likely both. Sometimes our effort to understand such flock-related matters is unsuccessful.

If hens—adults or young female turkeys—should breed unsuccess-fully, or not breed at all, they will gather in groups within that habitat and stay together through fall and winter. This dynamic creates the broodless flock. In such groups, female turkeys that are one-and-a-half years old by autumn (super jennies, if you will) stay together. Adult hens that nested unsuccessfully may be in this group, too. Again in late fall, you may also encounter a brood hen with female turkeys born that year, especially if growing fall jakes have left that family flock.

The adult longbeard is considered the ultimate challenge in the fall and winter turkey woods, but hunting a broodless hen or hens is equally difficult. It should be noted that a small percentage of female turkeys bear thin, wispy beards—one such example is accurately depicted by John James Audubon, I might add, in his version of a brood hen with poults. I've certainly seen them now and again over the years.

Unusual Flocks

As my then seven-year-old daughter told me: "Daddy, different people think different things." And if that isn't a statement for tolerance as turkey-hunting opinions go, I don't know what is. As an informed turkey hunter in the modern age, you need to tolerate certain camp storytellers who suggest fall gobblers don't gobble, that hens don't ever have beards, and that longbeards never travel with family flocks. They do, they do, they do. Think what you want, but unusual flocks are encountered each fall and winter.

Despite nature's effort to put young birds with brood hens and male gobblers with others of their kind, those of us who watch wild turkeys have seen flocks defying definition. I've witnessed adult autumn gobblers moving through the woods with family flocks, and seen combinations of

Solitary longbeards are the ultimate fall and winter turkey hunting challenge.
JOHN HAFNER PHOTO

brood hens, juveniles, and males in huge alliances. I've flushed an adult gobbler flock, only to see a single young turkey work to my calling. Given the complexity of the outdoor world, the ever-alert wild turkey will simply meet up with and spend time with others of its kind.

Often, turkey flocks grow larger and more diverse when a favored food source is both concentrated in one location and abundantly available. Scarce food sources cannot sustain a large flock, and groups must sometimes break up to create a more compatible unit for foraging. Flock combinations and associations can indeed be brief.

Solo Birds

It's clear that sometimes certain wild turkeys, like the New Hampshire gobbler I described, are alone in the woods, and prefer it that way. They run with no flock. They may or may not be adult birds. In some fall situations I've encountered a specific single bird in a particular habitat. It may be a turkey recently flushed by a predator or hunter, and as we might say in human terms, it's lost and separated from its flock. Or not. Armed with some of the calling information in chapter 6, you can address each situation based on the group of turkeys you find.

TEN FLOCK-BASED CALLING SITUATIONS

1. If a flockless individual turkey answers you in the woods while you cold call, imitate whatever call it makes. Cluck to a cluck. Match a gobbler yelp with a gobbler yelp. Mimic a kee-kee with a kee-kee. Don't get fancy. Imitate the solo bird.

2. If you know where the fall flock roosts and where they feed, set up early between the roost trees and the feeding zone. Either softly tree yelp right before or after the roosted birds begin calling or remain quiet until the flock begins to assemble after fly-down time.

3. If the family flock's brood hen begins to assembly yelp in an attempt to call young turkeys to that position, stand and slowly walk toward that bird. Ideally, she'll run off and stop calling for the moment. Return to your setup and resume calling, imitating the most vocal turkey in that family flock.

4. If you've flushed a male-only flock, set up at that spot until you're convinced they've regrouped. Hunt that day. Hunt the next. They may also return immediately, despite what you've read and heard elsewhere. Calling might begin with you making three coarse gobbler yelps. If it's a kee-kee-run you need to make, do that.

5. If you've poorly scattered flocked-up birds and they've simply flown into the trees above you, flush this flock again by walking under them. Find a good setup somewhere in the center of the departed birds, and call when turkeys begin talking again.

6. If a flock of turkeys is feeding toward you in a direct line as you slip undetected through the woods or fields, freeze. If you're standing close to the moving birds, lean against a concealing tree, your gun or bow ready. If the flock begins drifting off, you might be able to steer them in your direction with a soft cluck, yelp, kee-kee, or kee-kee-run after identifying flock composition.

7. If you've seen and heard a gobbler flock fighting to establish pecking order after fly-down, set up there early the next morning. At fly-down, call with fighting purrs, agitated clucks, yelps, and even gobbles. Have that gun on your knee or bow at your side for when that first red head periscopes in range.

8. If you've drawn an arrow and let it fly, missing the bird, sit tight. Slowly nock another arrow. If you've fired a load of pellets and whiffed, stay put. Be patient, even though frustration rises. A released arrow is obviously quieter than a gun blast. Call contentedly after the miss to assure turkeys all is well. The gun blast will have likely flushed birds, which you can later call back in to your position.

Yes, turkeys will come back to the same spot, even after the loud bark of a scattergun.

9. If in doubt, improvise. When bored with your setup, work on your calling. Empty the contents of your vest. Tune calls. Turkey sounds often chance at interesting roving flocks. Some might come in silently, so stay alert.

10. If you've given it a fair shot, and the wary fall or winter turkeys you've hunted have seen every trick in the calling playbook, find fresh birds. Turkeys don't ever really get call-shy, but they do feel the pressure of hunter effort. If time provides, scout to locate a new group of birds, preferably a flock that hasn't been hunted recently. Know when to focus on the intangible pleasure of the hunt and when to regroup to score.

TURKEY PREDATORS

Predation certainly influences flock size and composition. As individual birds and groups go, predation occurs in spring (on nesting hens) and summer (on poults). It also occurs in fall and winter, but less so as wild turkeys grow.

Egg eaters include crows, opossums, raccoons, feral dogs, foxes, and skunks, among various other creatures. Down south, certain snakes eat turkey eggs. Poult and juvenile turkey predators include hawks, big owls, foxes, coyotes, feral dogs, and bobcats, among others.

All predatory birds are protected by law, with the exception of crows, which can be hunted during specific seasons, depending on your state. Coyotes, foxes, raccoons, and bobcats can often be targeted as well. It's no coincidence that I've called coyotes into turkey setups in a handful of states over the years.

In the end, it's unsound wildlife habitat management and a difficult proposition to hunt predators excessively. They exist for a reason and help maintain balance in specific habitats. It should also be noted that as flock populations increase around the country, vehicular roadkills occur on major highways and back roads. Game laws ensure flock growth, and that benefits the turkey hunters.

CHAPTER 9

Mature autumn longbeards are the stuff of myth making during turkey-camp conversations. It's routinely suggested that fall adult gobblers are nearly impossible to kill, and maybe that's true for some hunters.

JOHN HAFNER PHOTO

Fall and Winter Gobblers

While I'm the first to argue "It's all good," I have endured agonizing stretches of time without tagging a wild turkey that have made me feel maybe the kill does matter a little. Okay, maybe a lot. Sometimes you have to risk that skunking to take a fall gobbler. You may pass on legal hens early and then find them scarce at the wire. As a result, you may even have to eat that turkey tag with barbecue sauce at the end of the season.

In the previous chapter, I discussed flock characteristics and how they change seasonally. Specifically hunting fall and winter gobblers involves targeting three kinds of birds within all-male groups: juvenile gobblers born that spring and summer, super jakes hatched the spring or summer the year before, and true longbeards over two years old. The birds-of-the-year are often slightly more abundant than the super jakes. The super jakes sometimes exceed the number of older sharp-spurred gobblers.

Again, some regions of the country—Missouri, Iowa, and certainly Texas—offer more surviving longbeard densities into autumn. Elsewhere, that's not the case. As a result, taking a male turkey born that year might be appropriate.

Turkey hunting is not only about acknowledging the tradition, but also adapting sporting practices to your own personal standards within specific game laws, which can vary widely from state to state. To those who prefer not to shoot fall hens even where it's legal, that might mean only taking younger male turkeys or tagging a longbeard for the ultimate challenge. To others, pulling the trigger on any either-sex legal bird could be the way to go.

Some regions of the country—Missouri, Iowa, and certainly Texas—offer more surviving longbeard densities into autumn.

To those who prefer not to shoot fall hens even where it's legal, that might mean only taking younger male turkeys or tagging adult gobblers for the ultimate challenge. Here, Virginians John Byrne and his son J. T. Byrne admire two autumn longbeards.

JAKES-OF-THE-YEAR

Identification rules if you want to take a growing gobbler instead of a juvenile hen. To distinguish a fall jake (a young male) from an autumn jenny (a young female), turkey hunters can focus on these specifics: face color, comparative physical characteristics, overall size, and vocalizations.

Face color: Jakes born that year often have recognizable pink faces by the time most autumn turkey seasons arrive. In shooting range, this quality can be seen as a skull-to-throat pink band that starts behind the beak and stops before the turkey's ear. If not, chances are it's a hen-of-the-year. Hens, both young and adult, have gray to grayish-blue faces. Hens tend to have more head feathering as well. Unlike the adult gobbler or super jake, a hen's head and face color will not change due to breeding or fighting mood. Yes, pink spots and coloring might be found on the necks of some hens but not usually around their eyes. As the young gobbler grows into winter, his head and neck become brick-red. Also, it's not uncommon for jakes to have red, white, and blue heads when aroused or strutting during their first attempts at breeding in spring.

Physical characteristics: Male bird breast feathers are black-tipped, while the hen's are brown-edged. By late fall and winter, males-of-the-year carry visible beards. I've found emerging $1/4$-inch beards hidden beneath the breast feathers of pink-faced jakes taken in early autumn. By winter, when the young male turkey is likely a half-year-old or so, the beard usually becomes visible to the onlooker, and as mentioned, the head has grown even redder. Tail fans are ragged on both young gobblers and hens. As other similarities go, both jakes and jennies born that year have brown legs, as opposed to the scaly pink legs of super jakes, year-and-a-half-old jennies, adult gobblers, and mature hens.

Size: Gobblers born that year are larger than the young hens from the same family flock. Depending on when their brood hatched, jennies tend to run six or seven pounds on average, while young jakes can run several pounds more in the heart of autumn and stand noticeably taller than their female flock mates. Smaller and larger weights might be noted. Even

Pink-faced jakes. Sure, they're just young gobblers, but they often provide exciting autumn and winter hunts. JOHN HAFNER PHOTO

when young, turkeys are large when compared to other gamebirds. By winter, the visual size difference between flock members is even easier to determine as turkeys grow.

Vocalizations: Beyond visual confirmation, the bird's vocalizations—specifically the familiar gobble—help with identification. (Isolated reports of a hen gobbling are rare indeed.) In fact, the fall jake's tendency to gobble—albeit a work in progress—adds to their appeal during autumn and winter hunts. While this young male turkey's voice might crack like any growing adolescent's, it's hard not to enjoy the full medley of a kee-kee-run followed by a rowdy gobble as you call autumn jakes to the gun.

SUPER JAKES

By definition, a gobbler under two years old is called a jake. Two kinds of jakes roam the fall and winter woods: the aforementioned pink-faced males that were born that particular year, and the super jake that hatched more than a year ago on the previous calendar.

Face color: Typically, the super jake's head and face are brick-red. His snood, the flap of flesh on the upper base of the turkey's beak, is often short and withdrawn during the fall and winter months. In spring, when gobblers are strutting—and when they're fighting—it dangles over the side of the male turkey's bill. When he struts in autumn to contest the pecking order, his head might turn red, white, and blue.

Physical characteristics: The beard of the super jake is usually more than five inches long (unless it's been damaged). His spurs are growing, but still just under an inch. Even his tail fan, which sported raised center primary feathers the past spring, is presentable now.

Size: He's still shy of two years, but the super jake exhibits similar physical features to a mature bird—there's no disputing his sex. On the check-in scale, he'll weigh sixteen to eighteen pounds on average.

Vocalizations: His gobble is mature and makes your hunter's heart bounce. His yelp is raspy. He clucks. He makes fighting purrs when contesting flock status.

One autumn, I encountered a flock of nine redheaded New York State super jakes, all of which had six- to seven-inch beards sprouting off their chests. Through the truck's grimy windshield, I watched them cross the dirt road from unposted land to boldly private property (no trespassing signs were nailed on fence posts every five feet or so). Can turkeys read? Sometimes I think so. At any rate, every fall I seem to run across a gang like this. And when found on land open to hunting, they offer plenty of sport.

Another fall season, two friends and I hunted a group of five super jakes after flushing them with dogs, legal in the Empire State. One bird returned to the break site after an hour or so and was taken. Another from the gobbler gang worked into range an hour or so after that, and it was dropped nearly in the same spot as the first bird. The third male turkey came in yet another hour later, clucking and gobbler yelping—unseen, seemingly suspicious, and just out of range. Well, two out of three ain't bad. Both of the New York gobblers we tagged in this team effort were nearly identical, sporting eight-inch beards, wearing spurs just shy of an inch, and weighing seventeen pounds and change.

Those jakes you chose not to shoot in spring because you were looking for an adult longbeard stay together into fall and create super-jake flocks. You could have had them for the taking back in spring, but in the five or six months since then, they've somehow grown warier. That's good, as the difficulty adds to the hunt.

The author's setter Midge standing guard with a gobbler that didn't get away.

TRUE LONGBEARDS

We all know him when we see him. My English setter Midge began yipping and barking at the top of a hilly bench, deep in the Catskills. Sure enough, a few turkeys alarm putted, then winged down the hill. They were big, black-feathered, and flew with flopping beards and extended red heads—a gobbler gang, for sure. I gathered my setter, loved her up a little, set up at the base of a broad oak, and let things calm down. To the turkey-dog man, a find and flock break like this is nearly equal to the kill.

Maybe twenty minutes later or so, I offered three raspy yelps on an old slate call. Bingo. A bird down the hill, obviously a gobbler by its response, mimicked my calling. I called, it answered, and soon I could hear it moving up the hill through the dry leaves, yelping to me as it came. I'd lay some silence on the bird, and then call again. The tom would answer right back. This was not the mature longbeard you read about that returns to the flush site a day later. This gobbler was coming in a hurry.

Gun up, Midge installed in her zippered camo bag, muzzle pointed in that bird's direction, I waited. Soon, the tom turkey's red head appeared at the other end of browned autumn goldenrod, maybe twenty steps away at most. Its beard was a solid ten inches. What a magnificent turkey. I centered the bead on its neck, and pulled.

Nothing. The tom, still seeking out the other bird I'd been imitating, moved to my right, craning its neck to see. Once again I aimed the pump gun, pulled the trigger, and heard silence. For the third time, I aimed (poorly, I might add), and fired—nothing, then something: the dysfunctional gun finally barked out a belated volley of copper-plated pellets. At that, the gobbler instantaneously lifted up and sailed back down the hill again. Miss. Game over, for now.

While this hunt might have been the low point in a season for some, there are highlights to note. First, my dog did a fine job. Second, my calling was competent enough to fool a mature autumn longbeard into gun range. Third, I can still see that gobbler in the middle of the night when sleep fails me, so at least I have a mental picture of it on file.

Face color: In spring, the adult gobbler's head will likely include blue around its beady black eye, a white cap on its head, a drooping snood when aroused, a blood-red and/or rosy-pink neck, with swollen bright-red caruncles at its base—a gaudy sight you love to see coming through the leafed-out woods. This head coloration is, of course, in dramatic contrast to the pink-faced, five-month-old fall jakes born in a particular year. I have also seen the red heads of autumn adult gobblers turn red, white, and blue when strutting or in a dominance posture before and during turkey fights.

Physical characteristics: As in spring, the autumn and winter tom might have just a single beard of nine to eleven inches on average, or multiple beards. These bristle-like growths, biology tells us, can technically be defined as feathering. My personal best carried three beards. A small percentage of hens also sport beards, though these growths are slimmer by comparison. Unlike the younger jake, the adult gobbler's spurs measure an inch or more. Its reptilian legs are pink.

Size: Let's just say its feet are big enough to support a large body that can weigh twenty pounds or more. This is the other mature tom that was standing next to the longbeard you shot last spring, now six months later.

Vocalizations: He gobbles, but not as much. He makes all the other turkey sounds you'd expect, but his head isn't clouded by the urge to breed. You can say his calling is highly selective. That's why he's such a challenge. Trust that if fresh ground sign is available (especially big-footed turkey tracks), the gobblers are out there—even if they choose to stay silent. Under such challenging conditions, you can hunt them based on sensible woodsmanship involving a variety of tactics shared in this book.

Mature autumn longbeards are the stuff of myth-making during turkey camp conversations, assuming they're talked about at all by the uninitiated. It's routinely suggested that fall adult gobblers are nearly impossible to kill, and maybe that's true for some hunters. Fall gobblers aren't interested in breeding, sure enough. They are gregarious, though. They are also focused on pecking order within the flock. Like any turkey, you can pattern them to gain an edge. Over the years, I have had reasonable success calling some memorable gobblers into range. Often the ones that got away, and it seems to happen more often than not in autumn, stick with me. In spring, a gobbler fixated on breeding can be an easy mark as he robotically works to your calling. Things change, come fall and winter.

CALLING FALL GOBBLERS

Clucking: When looking for flock mates, wild turkeys cluck. To make this sound on a slate, finger the peg with extra pressure, push down, and pull the tip toward you with a quick pluck. Gobbler clucks are usually low pitched. Find that sweet spot on your friction call's surface and cluck sparingly, pausing for several seconds or minutes between clucks.

Yelping: Gobbler yelps are deeper and have a slower cadence than higher-pitched hen yelps. They're also generally fewer in number. Again, friction calls imitate gobbler yelps best, though resonant diaphragms also

Quaker Boy's Dave Streb with an upstate New York October longbeard.

Let's just say its feet are big enough to support a large body that can weigh twenty pounds or more. This gobbler's spurs measured 1¹/₂ inches.

As in spring, the adult autumn and winter tom might have just a single beard of nine to eleven inches on average, or multiple beards.

work. Often three deeper, slower yelps—yawp, yawp, yawp—will get a super jake or mature gobbler's interest. Like the cluck, it's a questioning call that seems to say, "Where are you? I'm right here." As slate yelping goes, run your striker closer to the call's center than the rim. While holding the peg like a pen, draw it toward the call's middle with the one-two-three yelping rhythm of a gobbler. Experiment with strikers on your call of choice.

Gobbling: In the spring, a gobbler is primarily attempting to call hens to his roosted or ground-standing position. In the fall and winter, he's declaring his proud presence, and possibly gobbling during daily efforts to maintain pecking-order status, or move ahead in rank, as he fights other male birds. If you raise a gobbler with a cluck, then start yelping at the bird that responds to you, try gobbling at that turkey. Gobbler calls, when used sparingly, can draw responses from adult toms, super jakes, and young male turkeys. If you've broken the flock on foot, or with a dog, listen as the gobblers regroup. Often they'll gobble when lost or looking for other turkeys. Call as they do.

Fighting sounds: Aggressive purrs, cutting, and gobbling can interest male birds into approaching your position. Just as a crowd gathers during a street fight to see what's going on, gobblers will investigate the location where such sounds indicate fighting turkeys. You can hold the lid of your cap and smack it against a tree or your leg to imitate wings colliding as you purr, cutt, and gobble—so long as the turkeys are out of sight and won't chance at seeing your movements.

Note: Don't fall in love with your own calling. Use it as a tool and with deliberate purpose. Read the autumn and winter woods by listening and watching to know how long to wait before calling again. Make a move, pause, analyze the situation, let your feathered quarry do the same, and so on. Sometimes, too, you need to call in reinforcements involving several strategies.

WHEN IT WORKS

My buddy had scouted the Vermont property while bowhunting deer and had seen the gobbler gang. A mutual friend would take his turn at calling, and if luck prevailed, be the shooter. My setter Midge eventually found the longbeard flock then flushed it. After that, we set up and let the woods settle down. Clucks and gobbler yelps were offered from our position. To my left, I saw a dark figure pass, leaves crunching as it moved by. A regrouping longbeard was suddenly in range, there for the taking, but out of view to my hunting buddies. It drifted off, unimpressed at seeing no live bird where it continued to hear turkey sounds.

My friends hadn't seen the gobbler, so nothing was lost in the regret department. I still carried an unused tag in my wallet, but as a dog man, I'm often happy enough to take other hunters along in an effort to fill their tags. Shoot that fall longbeard? Hmm. Such dark moments haunt the inner thoughts of numbers-driven turkey hunters, but I'm happy to say that I did not have second thoughts. That's good, because the best was yet to come.

Not long after, another gobbler minced steps in to my left, even closer than the first turkey. As if extrasensory perception were kicking in—for neither of my two buddies had yet to see or hear a bird, I was later told—aggressive calling came from their position, with human-generated agitated purring and clucking punctuating the autumn air.

At that, the gobbler moved deliberately closer to them, hunching up in a fighting posture and striding in. Its head went from a brick-red to a dramatic red, white, and blue. It stopped. It clucked. A camouflaged shotgun barrel magically turned, adjusted its wavering length, and then barked an answer. Gobbler down. Hunt over. We shared high-fives all around, as my dog buried her face in the turkey's black-tipped breast feathers.

It had taken three men, a renegade English setter, and some ESP to tag that autumn Vermont longbeard.

CHAPTER 10

Fall flocks drift through habitats, often just out of gun and bow range. There's a safety zone wild turkeys are comfortable with. It's your job to sneak inside it and then flush those birds.

To Flush or Not to Flush?

In fall and winter turkey hunting circles, it's a given: when you break the flock up you gain an advantage. The wild turkey's desire to spend time with other flock members makes it possible to separate birds and then call scattered turkeys back to the gun or bow where you first found them. This enables you to vocalize to individual turkeys rather than entire groups.

OPTIONS, OPTIONS

You may ask: Why flush flocks at all? Why don't you just shoot a bird right then and there? The truth is, turkey flocks often move through habitats ahead of perceived danger. They are the essence of robotic wariness, often just out of gun and bow range. As you hunt through the woods, moving along trails and skirting fields, they're watching and listening. They'll drift steadily away to the next hillside, or one field over, often preferring to walk rather than take wing. There's a safety zone wild turkeys are comfortable with. It's your job to sneak inside it and then flush those birds.

The fall and winter turkey hunting tradition can involve one or all of the following flush-oriented strategies depending on where you hunt.

Pattern and Flush

You might pattern a flock, sit tight, wait to intercept that group, then flush them on foot—especially if they're walking just out of range. This often works well near funnels where birds enter fields to feed, or along game trails between roosts and food sources. After you scatter the flock, you can set up and call them back to the flush site. If the birds do arrive in range, of course, you can also just shoot one. Then again, you might choose to flush that flock just to make things interesting.

Walk Long and Far With Your Turkey Dog

Where legal, you might also cover a lot of ground in the big woods using a trained dog that scents, finds, and flushes flocks. If successful, you can then attempt to call those scattered turkeys back to the original flush site. This approach allows you to hunt on foot as you might other upland birds, walking a lot and enjoying the dog's company. Since you are covering a lot of ground looking for widely dispersed flocks, it's more interesting than just sitting in a blind and waiting for patterned turkeys to arrive. For those of us who like to walk a lot, hunting ridge tops, mountain hollows, and broad low-lying valleys with a canine is enjoyable. The turkeys might be tougher to pattern since you're often going into a new situation, a factor that adds to the hunt.

With or without the help of dogs, use woodsmanship to scout and hunt turkey habitat, noting signs of bird activity along the way, and actively listening for nearby flocks before hatching a strategy to separate them from each other.

Woodsmanship Works

Without the help of a dog, you might simply use woodsmanship to scout and hunt turkey habitat, noting signs of bird activity along the way and actively listening for nearby flocks before hatching a strategy to separate them from each other. Hunting new or proven ground on foot, you might piece the puzzle together on your own or do it with a buddy.

If hunting alone, you can either attempt to call those turkeys to your location if you hear them nearby—on roost before the morning fly-down, during the daytime, or as they head to roost in late afternoon. Tags providing, you can also take one of those birds if you get close enough, set up on those that scatter at the gunshot, and try to call another turkey back.

If you're hunting with a partner, one of you might take a turkey on the break, while another might set up after the gunshot (flushing birds a second time) and call one in that way. It's not foolproof, this scatter-and-call-back stuff. You might have some trouble closing the deal, especially if the break isn't effective.

GOOD AND BAD BREAKS

The objective to keep in mind in all cases is: if you flush them, they might come. A good break scatters individual turkeys in as many directions as possible. Single birds, separated from their flock mates, are often easier to call, and there's a high probability that you'll have at least some birds to work, though nothing surprises me as the turkey's inherent wariness goes. I've had good breaks turn bad as silent birds cagily regrouped, then moved off like smoke.

A bad break is an attempt to scatter flocked birds, only to watch small groups fly off together in several different directions. These mini-flocks are often content to stay together and won't always respond to the call-back. Other times you can pull in these smaller groups with your efforts. That's the fun of it. You're really in trouble if an attempt to flush a flock results in simply pushing the whole group in another direction. Alerted, you may never see them again that day.

To get a good break on foot, determine where you might sneak as close to a flock as possible. Use terrain to hide your movements, always wary of safety issues as such stalking goes. It's best to put your gun or bow where you might easily find it again, then do your best to sprint toward those turkeys.

Ideally, a group of turkeys busted in the woods will offer up the best break since the trees block their view of departing and remaining flock members. Flushing field turkeys has mixed results, as birds can track each other visually and stay together. Sometimes you get lucky with a big flock, though, where most of the birds stay together, but maybe a few

A bad break is an attempt to scatter flocked birds, only to watch small groups fly off together. These mini-flocks won't always respond to the callback. Other times you can pull in these smaller groups with your efforts. The author snapped this quick picture after rushing an early October family flock inside edge cover.

move off in the other direction. Target those few turkeys in your follow-up calling effort.

Noise helps. I've shouted when rushing flocks, barked like a dog, and clapped my hands to get them in the air. Some hunters have decent success scattering birds with a gunshot pointed in a safe direction. This can be especially effective if you find yourself on a ridge top above a flock that's moving and feeding below you in a wooded hollow. For some reason, the loud bark of a gun from above makes turkeys flush in all directions.

No matter which method you employ, make an effort to follow up flushes to ensure nearby turkeys in trees fly off again—hopefully even further away from other departed birds. This post-scatter method offers a little additional insurance. Walk around the general area of the flush site, pausing and looking for turkeys in trees. Now and then you'll hear or see one winging off. Don't worry—they'll be back.

Maybe. Nothing's foolproof. On some occasions, you may get a good break, but the turkeys might still succeed in getting back together after that initial flush. If you have a dog along, the flock can be dispersed

On buddy hunts, you can double-team birds by splitting up, then moving at the turkeys from different directions. In such situations, caution is in order. Set up a plan before you advance on the flock, and stick to it.

again. If you're on foot, you may have to start from scratch, relocating the flock, and rushing them again. On buddy hunts, you can double-team birds by splitting up, then moving at the turkeys from different directions. In such situations, caution is in order. Set up a plan before you advance on the flock, and stick to it. Decide whether or not you'll shoot one on the flush if the opportunity presents itself. Use a crow call or some other natural game-call device to communicate your location to each other.

No matter what you do, the turkeys may still win. At times, it's amazing how a once rowdy flock of vocal turkeys can go silent post-flush and vaporize in the fall woods. That's why they call them wild.

FALL FLUSHING TIPS
Find where flocks roost and feed. Realize that flushing turkeys on their way between these two locations is an option, not a necessity. To sneak close to a flock before flushing them, listen for turkey vocalizations such as purring and clucking, as well as scratching in the leaves. Move slowly on turkey time. Get ahead of moving groups if you can, after determining

WINGSHOOTING TURKEYS

Most of the time it's best to call a wild turkey into range and then squeeze off a shot aimed at the standing bird's head and neck. Though it's not the best way to anchor a fall or winter gobbler or hen, the opportunity to wingshoot a turkey might present itself—especially on the flush. It's a controversial subject, for sure. Still, autumn and winter situations often make it possible to take a turkey on the wing.

In most upland hunting circles, it's sporting to shoot nearly all gamebirds in the air after flushing, rather than on the ground the way we do wild turkeys. Why do we reverse this for the latter bird? How can you avoid crippling turkeys?

As with upland bird hunting, it's crucial that you mount the shotgun properly, and that you push your cheek to the gunstock. When shooting flying turkeys, it's important that you only aim for the head and neck. Even better, shoot for the beak. Body shots are to be avoided.

The question is: are you a confident wingshooter? If so, shooting an occasional fall or winter turkey in flight might be feasible. If not, stick with calling a bird into range on the ground and shooting that bird cleanly. Shooting flying gobblers or hens in season isn't for everyone, but every veteran fall and winter turkey chaser knows the situation presents itself now and again in flushing situations.

In truth, it's hard to judge range on flying turkeys, and since body shots are out, most opportunities should be passed up. If a dog is pursuing a flock in a flush situation, I'd strongly recommend against shooting flying turkeys, unless you see that head and neck extended on a particular bird, and blue (or gray) sky behind it. Always check first for the dog's location. Always.

Hunters can make good shots by estimating how close the departing turkey might be and if that bird is in gun range. A good judging point is to fixate on the bird's black eye. Again, while you might shoot into the air to get a good flock break, this doesn't always mean you should pull the trigger on a departing bird as it takes wing. Use good judgment.

The likely potential for crippling losses where the airborne wild turkey is hit, but doesn't die immediately should be a deterrent. That body-shot bird might be far from recovery.

Maybe you've called a turkey into range and shot at it. If that crippled bird is trying to take wing, another shot is definitely in order. Maybe you spooked a wild turkey on a game trail while moving through the woods. If that bird is in range, a wingshot might prove successful. Turkey size varies in the fall, from smaller hens to full-grown gobblers. At times, shooting a juvenile turkey on the wing is a more reliable option than trying to down a sturdy, well-built longbeard.

In the end, the decision is personal. Clean kills on turkeys should be the aim. Most of the time it's better to call one up into range, then drop the turkey as it stands there. Period.

which direction they're working in. Your goal is to flush every turkey in that flock in a different direction. Position yourself to do that.

A trained dog will give you the advantage of flushing more effectively. This advantage is often balanced out when you try to hide that wriggling setter in the blind as turkeys regroup. Still, roving fall flocks can be tough to find, with or without a canine's help.

What if you miss a turkey in range as flock members regroup? Sit tight, and don't dwell on the whiff. As in baseball, that's just one strike against you. Sometimes such a shot flushes other nearby birds in several directions. Chances are you can set up to call them back in again after the woods settle down, or you can simply stay put. Other birds might still be working toward your position.

Flushing birds and calling scattered turkeys back is exciting stuff. Before moving to a new hunting area, always check your calling setup with a glance to see if you've left any of your gear behind. Many times a quick look will reveal a pair of gloves or that prized friction call still sitting there on the ground.

CHAPTER 11

Wild turkeys know where they want to go. You need to figure out how they get there, from fly-down to fly-up.

JOHN HAFNER PHOTO

Patterning Turkeys

Wild turkeys know where they want to go.
You need to figure out how they get there, from fly-down to fly-up. While scouting is noting the presence of turkeys, patterning is an effort to determine their movements. Knowing the habitat you hunt helps you to tell how wild turkeys might move about. Terrain dictates wild turkey movements. It limits their range. It increases it. You need to decode autumn and winter flock activity based on the topography of the land. Remember, patterns change as well, and you need to adapt.

Walk with your head up as you scout. And down. Looking for turkey sign with your eyes to the ground is required, for sure. Also make certain you scan the habitat ahead to see the big picture, moving slowly through cover, watching pasture corners and other access points. A flock might be there. This studying process takes time and can't be rushed. The more you scout the land you hunt, the better you'll be at deciphering turkey movements.

As you pattern birds, avoid affecting their routine, which chances at altering their daily movements. Given the situation, arrive early in the woods to see where they roost, where they fly down, then where they go. Spend the day there, or at least a portion of it, listening and watching for turkeys. Leave by flashlight after dark at the end of the day if fall and winter flocks are nearby in late afternoon. Integrate yourself into the woods.

Ideally, you should move slowly through the land you are scouting or hunting. Don't rush. Look. Listen. Take some deep breaths. Slow down. Sit. Read a book while watching a field. Nap in the warm October sun if it keeps you there. It's one thing to know established property lines—

landmarks such as fences, food sources, streams, swamps, pasture fields, ridge tops, farmhouses, barns, and so on—but it's also crucial that you see the details inside the general picture.

Devote enough time on a regular basis to study how birds move during the day. Note any changes that occur in the travels of turkeys and why that shift might have happened. As always, watch for ground sign in the form of fresh tracks, droppings, scratchings, and so on.

Phases of turkey movement are sometimes predictable. Active periods occur after the morning fly-down time, when birds are likely to hit a food source. Flocks tend to loaf and dust midday. Movement might be minimal. In mid to late afternoon, birds move about again and feed actively.

I honestly believe wild turkeys can pattern us at times—especially when we repeatedly visit an area they inhabit. Have you ever had a turkey flush at extremely close range as you moved through the woods? Have they done it more than once? Have you ever thought a flock wasn't in a field, only to have those birds emerge from a hedgerow after you've passed and looked back? Have you ever seen a hen squat down in tall pasture grass and flatten herself into the shape and color of a cow pie?

Walk with your head up as you scout. And down. Looking for turkey sign with your eyes to the ground is required, for sure. Also make certain you scan the habitat ahead to see the big picture, moving slowly through cover, watching pasture corners and other access points. A flock might be there.

Have you ever seen an entire group of big birds disappear in a field of goldenrod?

I think that when wary turkeys get tough to pattern and hunt, they've noted our movements and sense something isn't right. That's why integrating yourself into their world as discretely as possible is key.

MOUNTAINS, HILLS, AND RIDGE TOPS

Mountain flocks roam widely in fall, especially if food sources are varied and dispersed, as they tend to be in such habitats. Hillside roosts are often favored during calmer autumn days, where turkeys feed after fly-down, while sheltered hollows below these spots will hold birds during blustery days and nights. Ridge tops that afford a view in all directions coupled with a food source such as acorns or beechnuts often hold turkey flocks. Certain flocks favor spots sloping down toward a flat bottom, where turkeys might wing off more readily on perceiving danger.

Such terrain makes wary birds difficult to approach from below, unless you do so in the dark. If scouting or hunting these areas by day, move in such a way that you won't alarm them. Pattern them by spending time in that rugged location, then hunting there the next day after you've fixed bird movements. Get in early, and stay all day if you can. Sometimes it takes all season to get a sense of how flocks are moving.

OPEN FIELDS, PASTURES, AND VALLEYS

Open fields, pastures, and valleys are refuges for flocks that provide both food and safety from approaching danger. Turkeys will often favor a certain corner game trail or funnel to enter such spots. Find these entryways, and you may solve at least a piece of the patterning mystery. Access areas vary. A break in the hogwire fencing that permits animals to move to and from open fields and pastures will often see turkey movement. And despite what some say, certain wild turkeys will fly over fences, while others will puzzle over the stationary impediment. Think like a turkey. Ask yourself, "What would a turkey do here?"

Often autumn and winter flocks will choose to enter a field via an elevated rise. This prey species must keep a constant eye on the nearby surroundings, and walking the higher area of a field gives turkeys this edge. As a result, this might also be the same area where you see a spring gobbler strutting.

Hunters should also note where hilly terrain and open fields converge to form a valley, as wild turkeys will often move regularly through the woods, along edge cover, and through a long narrow lowland to a field, then back again to roost in a regular pattern. If they do it on consecutive days, be there the next morning. You've patterned them.

Grasshoppers and alfalfa greens filled this Vermont fall turkey's throat crop, definitive evidence of preferred food sources.

SWAMPS

Gray pools of standing water. Spanish moss. Cypress trees as old as our hunting tradition. Armadillos scurrying in the dry leaves. Such places can be strangely beautiful to wild turkey hunters, as swampy habitats are home to many southern turkey flocks.

Elsewhere around the country, too, turkeys often choose roosting trees above swamps and standing water. To pattern birds in such terrain it's important to distinguish dry land from damp. Obviously flocks will move through areas such as dry hardwoods more readily than gator-lurking backwaters. Walk the land yourself. Experience it as a turkey does. It's not uncommon for swamp flocks to wade through shallow water. Others will fly to dry land from a water-encircled roost each early morning, and from it in late afternoon as a kind of launch pad. Find the general location where birds congregate before elevating to and from their sleeping spots in swamps, and you've isolated another piece of the patterning puzzle.

KNOW YOUR BIRDS

Revisiting flock types for a moment, you'll generally pattern three groups in the autumn woods:

1. Family flocks with brood hens and juvenile turkeys of both sexes.
2. Broodless hen groups.
3. Gobbler gangs (including jake-only flocks).

Any other fall mixed-flock combinations are incidental and are likely due to limited food sources or habitat, or both. By winter, you may find massive flocks that include these three groups, especially if food sources are limited. Occasionally, a wild turkey will be traveling alone too.

Though it's possible to find an autumn gobbler gang and family flock in the same pasture, generally each group keeps its distance from the other one. Broodless females, for instance, aren't driven to take care of young (since they have none). As a result, it's best to think of the gobbler gang and broodless group of hens in a similar way. Neither tends to juvenile birds, and both are more concerned about their own immediate survival. On the other hand, a biologically driven brood hen will often risk life and wing to protect her flock.

Jakes also appear together in woods and fields come late fall and early winter, especially if flock harmony is disrupted by their rage for pecking order status. For a time before the formation of these gangs of young male turkeys, jakes may even dominate a family flock. You'll occasionally notice this in a call-back, post-flush hunting situation, or after flydown time, as a single dominant jake may kee-kee-run, yelp, and gobble flock mates to its position, much as the brood hen might remain in a fixed spot while making its assembly yelp. If you haven't noticed this flock dynamic, then you aren't spending enough time with fall and winter turkeys. These social groupings are important to note as you pattern birds. In a given habitat, you may be scouting several flocks with varying movement tendencies.

TRACKING TURKEYS

Fresh snow is great if weather provides, as it enhances the recent tracks of birds, while sub-freezing nights lock old footprints in icy imagery that tells you turkeys passed through there at some point. When? You'd have to recall weather patterns and then guess at it. Muddy trails obviously carry the evidence, too. Pattern turkeys by noting regular use of such spots. If tracks continue to be fresh from day to day, you've successfully marked their movements.

Tracking can be an integral part of many fall and winter turkey hunts, and it's definitely an underappreciated hunting tactic. While both snow and mud carry tracks, a pattern of scratchings in the woods, especially if fresh, can also allow you to trail turkeys.

Always remember to follow the actual movements of fall and winter birds based on fresh tracks and scratchings, and not your preferred path of least resistance, though they sometimes simply move along the same acorn-strewn logging trail you prefer to walk. It's not uncommon for turkeys to ramble off-trail, through areas of vegetation and into denser thickets.

If you track turkeys one day in a particular location, you may have patterned them for the next morning. Get in there early, and install yourself near fresh tracks. After this, calling or simply waiting there for turkeys to arrive might result in you slipping a bird into your field vest.

FOOD PLOTS

Where available, wild turkeys feed on natural sources such as seeds and berries, beechnuts, acorns, and a widespread variety of other options. Before the first hard frost, family flocks may roost near field edges where bug-rich vegetation is present—even after, as the deep chill will often immobilize some insects, making them ripe for the picking. A gobbler gang or other flock of turkeys may routinely lurk near a farmer's edge-cover manure pile in search of waste corn and worms. Landowners can also hold birds on their property by developing food-rich locations. They can cultivate their holdings to draw turkeys.

The wild turkey's extensive diet offers landholders many options for planting food to attract flocks. Some of the more popular plantings

Fresh snow is great if weather provides, enhancing the recent tracks of birds. Once turkeys are patterned, where legal you can use a dog to flush the flock as it enters a predicted location.

include grain- or seed-bearing crops, legumes, clover, fruit-bearing bushes, and insect-attracting weeds and grasses. Many manufactured turkey food mixes produced specifically to sustain wild birds contain combinations of seeds to keep plots active year-round, with plants maturing at different times during the season. This is the same model often used by wildlife managers on state properties openly developed and maintained for hunting.

Geographical regions present various options. Warm-weather locations for plantings can include chufa, legumes, sorghum, and millet. In colder climates with greater seasonal changes, wheat, vetch, oats, various clovers, rye, and corn are some of the species used to attract and support wild turkeys. Oats, in fact, are a good planting specifically for turkeys, as deer will sometimes ignore this offering.

Planted clover can provide bug-rich habitat for summertime and early autumn family flocks, and in places that will likely hold fall and winter turkeys. Chufa yields subsurface tubers, which turkeys like to scratch up and eat. Millet attracts not only turkeys, but other upland birds such as quail, dove, and pheasant. Sunflowers, which mature during the warmer months, drop seeds that many birds relish. When intentionally planted in conjunction with millet—which matures faster than sunflower—you can create a one-two punch for fall turkeys. In places like the Midwest, Mid-Atlantic States, and New England, corn provides sustenance for wild turkey flocks.

As late autumn approaches, northern turkey flocks often rely on leftover grain in harvested fields. Landowners can also leave standing rows of corn near areas of mature timber to attract birds. Once, on a Pennsylvania fall turkey hunt, my hunting buddies and I watched as a huge flock filed out of and bolted from standing corn like ants shooed from a picnic table. They were in there and we didn't even know it. We'd seen plenty of sign, but little did we suspect that they were inside the rows of corn.

For long-term annual food production, hardwood trees such as hickory and oak are desirable for turkeys. Soft-mast trees such as wild plums, crabapple, wild cherries, flowering dogwood, and persimmon are popular choices, too.

Plot design can influence how turkeys utilize property. Some food plots might be smaller than an acre. Others can be three to four acres or more. In many cases, food plots should be established to border mature woods—often near a source of fresh water. Wooded edge cover provides wild turkeys with a quick escape if necessary.

Put simply, patch cuts (removing trees from a small area of woods) can be made to facilitate forested openings. This can provide additional growing room for existing trees, and it encourages the ongoing regeneration of acorn-bearing oaks and nut-producing hickories for wild turkeys. In northern regions, planted openings provide areas where insects congregate on plants and weeds in summer and early fall before the wave of killing frosts arrives. Elsewhere, protein-rich bugs linger as long as warm weather does.

Once food plots are established, landowners might wish to cut travel lanes to and from these areas, a common practice at state-owned wildlife management areas around the country. Such trails can be easily maintained by mowing, and both turkeys and deer will use them to come and go.

Fall and winter turkeys move to find food. In times of scarcity, they'll cover a lot of ground. Cultivated plots will attract roving birds from great distances and then hold them. Travel lanes to food plots can aid flock movements from roosting to feeding zones in the morning and allow them to feed late in the afternoon before traveling back to the roosting trees. As a result, landowners can pattern these turkeys on a daily basis, as they might when scouting or hunting deer. Flocks will visit areas with a general routine, perhaps even arriving the same time daily—likely early and late in the day. Though fall and winter turkeys roam widely, if they aren't in the trees by night, or held there during daytime stormy stretches, they're obviously somewhere else.

BLINDS

You can hunt turkeys two ways after you've patterned them. You can get out there and target them along the course of their daily travels, or you can establish a blind in range of where you expect them to arrive at a given time and sit there, waiting.

Some landowning hunters establish blinds near food plots, often where travel lanes converge, near access points—a tactic like that used by deer hunters in some parts of the country. Position these camouflaged setups based on a sense of game movement. Some hunters might wish to sit patiently, in silence, for the turkeys to arrive. Others might prefer to call in hopes of interesting nearby birds.

The waiting game often works if you have a young hunter or person new to the tradition along. A blind will help conceal errant or intended movements. Placed near a manmade food plot or in a natural travel lane, blinds provide a kind of sanctuary where you can sit, read, eat, nap, or whatever, and still be hunting turkeys. It's also good if you have a physically challenged buddy along who wants to hunt in a stationary location. Blinds can be an especially effective tool if you're trying to take your turkey with archery tackle, as your draw and release actions must be hidden.

Some camouflage blinds afford more mobility and can be erected quickly. Other hides are intended to be more stationary. Most have windows, often on each side. Many even fold up into carry bags. Once integrated into the location you intend to hunt, a blind can let you come and go as you please during the day, affording quick hunts.

MAPS

Maps. Turkey hunters love them. Maps are mounted to camp walls, carried in vests, and stashed in truck cab compartments. Maps are scrawled on diner napkins by landowners offering use of their property. Maps are often memorized and carried in our heads. The modern turkey camps I've visited around the country often use computer mapping software and aerial photographs.

Maps. Turkey hunters love them. Maps are mounted to camp walls, carried in vests, and stashed in truck cab compartments. Whatever maps you choose, it's important to still get out there and match your scouting experience with what you see on paper.

Maps are often memorized and carried in our heads. The modern turkey camps I've visited around the country often use computer mapping software and aerial photographs.

Whatever maps you choose, it's important to still get out there and match your scouting experience with what you see on paper. No matter what terrain you hunt them in, or what strategy you use, developing a sustained relationship with a particular group of turkeys (or even a single bird) is suggested. In order to turn general speculation about flock movements into something more than guesswork, go out alone, all day if you can. Do it on consecutive days. Patterning turkeys using woodsmanship is an acquired skill. It has to be earned.

CHAPTER 12

Wild turkeys live with the weather, like it or not. How they react in certain conditions determines how you hunt them.

JOHN HAFNER PHOTO

Weather or Not

Wild turkeys live with the weather, like it or not. How they react in certain conditions determines how you hunt them. If rainfall is heavy at fly-down time, turkeys might stay right on their tree branches. If rain arrives after flocks are on the ground, birds will more than likely move to open fields or edge cover. Weather extremes can definitely alter daily turkey patterns.

WIND AND RAIN

During one of my rainy-day autumn road trips, I arrived late for fly-down in a mature upstate New York oak stand—or so I thought. As I scanned the mid-morning woods below for bird activity, having slipped in there quietly with damp leaves underfoot, I felt something watching me. A super jake with a seven-inch beard looked down, no more than twenty yards away, craning its long neck at the camouflaged interloper. In domino-effect succession, it winged off with four other still-roosted male turkeys, and I never did hear from those birds again.

During another fall downpour while simply driving around looking for local field birds, I spotted a stationary red blotch daubed on top of what appeared to be a black overcoat draped on a low-lying bush along edge cover: a weird image. Was this a decorated Halloween dummy? Binoculars told me otherwise: the turkey, a mature, hunched-over gobbler, had its serpentine neck and head tucked under a protective wing, like a feathery umbrella. The bird didn't move. Returning to the area later in the day after the rain subsided, I found the turkey gone.

On both occasions, heavy rain kept turkeys in concealing cover. On the other hand, showery or drizzly days see plenty of flock activity. Such weather events actually seem to flush birds out of the woods and into

Heavy rain can keep wild turkeys in concealing cover. On the other hand, showery, misty, drizzly days can see plenty of flock activity. Such weather events actually seem to flush birds out of the woods and into open areas. Scouting or hunting during these foul-weather days can spell success.

open areas. Scouting or hunting fields, pastures, prairies, and other open spaces during these foul-weather days can spell success.

Turkeys look. Turkeys listen. Wind makes it tough for them to do both. Wind-tossed tree branches make the woods a place of constant motion. There's often enough noise to challenge a turkey's hearing, and prey species require that ability. As a result, flocks often move to calmer locations. Hollows, draws, and places out of the wind will get their attention on such days. If a food source is also available there, turkeys may linger in that location. A combination of steady wind and rain will definitely push them into these spots.

And it's not just turkeys that have trouble hearing on windy days. You will also find it difficult, if not impossible, to hear birds. It's tough to enjoy all that a calling session can offer with gusts whipping past your ears. You can combat this by calling loudly, hoping that a turkey in earshot will come drifting in or that an entire flock might get curious. Sometimes you might just be able to pick out a single calling turkey as the wind ebbs and flows past your position. Key on that bird, and call it in.

Snow helps you track turkeys.

On a positive note, windy days are more forgiving as hunter movement goes. You can get away with more while on the move looking for turkeys and while at your setup position.

WINTER WEATHER

Snow helps you track turkeys. Heavy snow may limit your ability to find birds though, as flocks are likely to remain stationary, staying on the roost. Assuming temperatures are moderate, light snow hardly impacts them at all, and is definitely preferred by hunters and their quarry.

Severe winters with lingering snow cover can affect turkey populations. Turkey movement is often impacted dramatically. Starvation is the greatest challenge in northern locations. Often flocks will shift range from a higher to lower elevation as a result, seeking out food sources for survival. Out west, big turkey flocks routinely mingle with livestock during harsh winter periods. It's not uncommon here in the Northeast to hear winter reports of turkey flocks regularly visiting backyard birdfeeders as well.

Powdered snow also challenges turkeys, as it inhibits their ability to walk to food sources. A foot of fluffy snow can limit most turkey movement. Packed and crusted snow cover is often better, as they can walk on top of it. Deep snow, whether it's powder or packed, makes it difficult for turkeys to eat.

In the end, the omnivorous wild turkey can endure severe winter weather if nutritional needs are met. Agricultural lands in turkey country with standing corn, waste grains, and wooded locations with spring seeps where surface-flowing groundwater and winter sun melts snow, sustain birds.

Fog can help you sneak closer to flocks. It also impacts a wild turkey's ability to see great distances, so dense fog may sometimes keep them on the roost. Fog following rain may actually increase turkey movement, as birds transition between roosts and open areas where they preen and feed. If the sun peeks out after a steady rain then foggy stretch, get to nearby open areas as soon as possible. The turkeys should be there.

EXTREME TEMPERATURES

Turkeys are tough. Cold combined with heavy snow is more challenging than just sub-freezing temperatures. The lower the air temperature goes, the greater the stress on all wildlife, including turkeys. Predators are

In the end, the omnivorous wild turkey can endure winter weather if nutritional needs are met. Wooded locations with spring seeps, where surface-flowing groundwater and winter sun melts snow, sustain birds. JOHN HAFNER PHOTO

Agricultural lands in turkey country with standing corn and waste grains help turkeys navigate winter.

always nearby in such situations, ready to play that advantage into a meal. Steady winds and low temperatures combined with winter ice storms can cause some turkeys to die of exposure.

Early-season fall days can sometimes resemble a lingering version of summer. Texas and desert southwest birds live out their feathered lives in such rising-mercury extremes and seem just as active and vocal during hot spells as on cooler days, unaffected by the heat. In areas where food sources don't provide adequate moisture (insects offer some), turkeys will regularly visit water holes during their daily rounds. I've taken Rio Grande turkeys over the years when the temperature was higher than 80 degrees. Sometimes they're vocal; sometimes they're not.

It's often different in northernmost regions, where early-fall weather extremes shut down turkey talk and flock movement. The birds are out there, but are sometimes unresponsive and may simply be biding their time in shaded cover. Then again, sudden warm days in the dead of winter will often increase turkey activity dramatically.

DANGEROUS WEATHER
Tornado warnings. Hollywood thunder. Jagged lightning. Gusts that blew my hat off a time or two. Heavy rain. I saw it all one Missouri morning. At least I took comfort in the fact that my epitaph could have read: Steve Hickoff, Killed While Turkey Hunting.

The roosted wild turkeys roughly fifty yards from my setup waited for a break in the weather, then flew down to the middle of a big, open field, and ran—I'm serious—to a big hedgerow-protected slot in the pas-

SOME BAD WEATHER TURKEY TIPS

- On windy days, look for turkey flocks in fields and open hollows. Don't squander hunting time elsewhere.
- Many manufacturers offer waterproof friction calls. Of course, mouth diaphragms work no matter what the weather.
- Sleep in on extreme weather days, estimating when the storm will break. Plan on hitting the woods when that window of time arrives.
- Use online sources to predict weather patterns such as www.accuweather.com and www.intellicast.com, including radar tracking available at such sites.
- Dress for success. Wear wind- and water-resistant clothing to keep you outdoors when everyone else has given up. Carry a change of dry camouflage clothing in a plastic container in your vehicle as well.

On windy days, look for turkey flocks in fields and open hollows.
Don't squander hunting time elsewhere.

ture where they stood in the diminishing showers but steady wind, shaking off the rain like a gang of black Labs during a flooded timber duck hunt. I had to laugh at that. Later that afternoon in another location, I did manage to tag a turkey—a bird that was simply drying off in yet another wide-open, semi-protected location and got just curious enough to mince steps into range.

Good, bad, or downright ugly, flocks are out there in that weather, so you might as well be, too. Personally, I love it all—warm October sunlight falling on stone pasture walls as I sit and take it all in, the whisper of yellow and red hardwoods nearby, the fragrant smell of woodlot leaves in decay, the raw feeling of snow flurries on breezy mountain ridges, and even cold November rains that shut everything down and put you behind a camp window with a cup of black coffee in your hands, especially with the promise of turkeys nearby when it clears.

Perception is certainly part of understanding how weather patterns affect flocks, but it's clear that sometimes turkeys will do just as they please, weather or not.

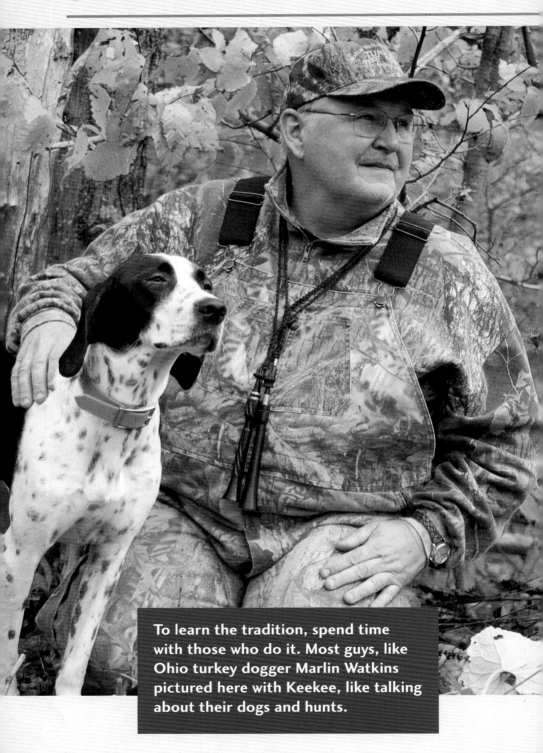

CHAPTER 13

To learn the tradition, spend time with those who do it. Most guys, like Ohio turkey dogger Marlin Watkins pictured here with Keekee, like talking about their dogs and hunts.

The Turkey Dogging Tradition

Up ahead, a graceful snow-white dog flashes through an October shower of sunlight, as red and yellow leaves slowly fall. Tail moving like a windshield wiper, head down like a hound, the canine scours the hillside for turkey scent, and then she's suddenly out of sight. Her sharp barking is followed by alarm putts as wild turkeys run and flush in all directions. You hustle ahead as several birds claw through the treetops with their wing beats. Several more sprint ahead, then out of view—heavy bodies wobbling away on skinny legs. In shotgun range, a few lingering turkeys, still as staked decoys, stand puzzled . . . that is, until your canine hunting partner runs them off, too. Mission accomplished. Success is at hand.

After selecting a setup spot near the flush site where you both can settle in comfortably, you construct a makeshift blind of deadfall, tangled branches, and fallen leaves. You pull some rolled-up camouflage burlap from your vest and shape that around the hideaway. You whistle the dog back from where she noses up the lingering turkey scent then show her a little love. "Good girl," you praise her. "Good girl." You slip her into a zippered, leaf-patterned cloth bag made for such occasions, and then gently cover the top of the dog's head so that only her half-closed eyes and muzzle are seen on your occasional glances. You lean back against a broad tree trunk. You wait, listening.

Shy of an hour later, one turkey kee-kee-runs in front of your position, and your heart leaps just a little. Your dog stirs and you calm her.

The author and his English setter Midge with two hard-won upstate New York fall turkeys.

Another turkey responds, and you hear footsteps approaching to your right. With a double-reed mouth diaphragm, you mimic the lost calls of both birds. They answer, draw closer. Sweet minutes pass.

As spokes angle to a wheel's hub, turkeys begin to come in from all directions. Suddenly, a juvenile gobbler appears, nearly in range, weaving toward your position. This dark-bodied jake boldly cranes its brick-red reptilian head, then barks: "kee-kee-kee-yawp, yawp, garobble."

As the turkey warily passes behind a broad oak, you raise your shotgun, swiftly and surely. The bird stops, sensing your presence. You aim down the barrel at where it will step out from behind the tree and then, targeting its head and neck when it does, respond with a single, clean shot. Your dog vaults from your setup and runs to the downed turkey. You instinctively check your firearm's safety and then take a deep breath and smile. Your dog buries her face in the scent of the downed bird. Far off, the calls of regrouping turkeys continue. You tag the bird, let your canine bud have one last sniff, and move down the ridge to the truck.

THE ORIGINS OF TURKEY DOGGING
All sporting traditions start somewhere, and turkey dogging emerged during that time when all manner of hunting approaches were permitted.

Nowadays, our pursuit of gobblers and hens is strictly regulated. As with other strategies employed in the autumn and winter turkey woods, there's an inherent sense of fair chase and sportsmanlike conduct.

Pursuing wild turkeys with dogs has a literary history as well, albeit selective. Evidence of American turkey dogging can be traced to the nineteenth-century writings of Audubon, as well as McIlhenny and Jordan, who reflected this approach in their book, *The Wild Turkey and Its Hunting* (1914), devoting an entire chapter to the subject of hunting turkeys with dogs. Henry E. Davis's *The American Wild Turkey* (1949) also included turkey dogging commentary in his chapter on hunting methods. The modern turkey dogger can read this historical writing and note both contrasting outdated perspectives, as well as strategies that are both legal and viable today.

Wild turkey management in the mid to late twentieth century involved a variety of approaches—from naively experimental to biologically substantive—as bird populations plummeted before conservation-oriented restoration efforts increased flock numbers nationally (only Alaska is currently without turkey flocks). This positive trend made it

In the early 1990s, eleven states permitted turkey hunting with dogs. Today, the number of places where the dogging strategy is legal has more than doubled as turkey populations continue to exceed original historical ranges.

Why flush wild turkeys with a dog? Four-legged hunting companions simply do it better than you can, assuming they're trained to the task. Pictured here, the author's wife Elizabeth Edwards with her first wild turkey, taken on a fall hunt with dogs.

possible to introduce both new spring and fall/winter seasons, including opportunities for dogs.

When I first chased New York State fall flocks with a canine in the early 1990s, some eleven states permitted turkey hunting with dogs. Today, the number of places where the dogging strategy is legal has more than doubled as turkey populations continue to exceed original historical ranges. (A complete list is included in the "Fall and Winter Where-To" chapter.)

For the serious enthusiast, contemporary turkey dogging has enormous appeal. A loss in one hunting situation is a measure of success in another. For instance, in many forms of upland hunting, you rely on a well-heeled dog to indicate the presence of birds without alerting that quarry. As the handler, you decide when that should be done with verbal or whistled commands, hand signals, body language, or all three. Should that canine move winged game well ahead of your shotgun, your heart typically sinks—a blown opportunity. However, if you're hunting fall and winter turkeys, a renegade dog flushing a flock is cause for celebrating.

Why flush wild turkeys with a dog? Four-legged hunting companions simply do it better than you can, assuming they're trained to the task. Admit it. The prospect of you lurching and stumbling toward a group of

Turkey dogging is often permitted where other upland bird seasons coincide. Radar, one of the author's English setters, sits with a brace of rooster pheasants.

wild turkeys with a loaded shotgun is not an effective proposition. Yes, it can be done. You can put your firearm down in a place you'll be sure to find it again, use concealing terrain to sneak closer to the group, then rush the birds to get a good break. No matter how well you separate flocks, though, a dog is likely to ace your turkey-flushing efforts.

In truth, there's just something about hunting wild turkeys with a dog that's flat-out appealing. As a viable tradition, it combines the companionship and trained skills that gun-dog enthusiasts enjoy when pursuing such species as grouse, woodcock, quail, and pheasant, while also including the fall and winter turkey hunting component. There's a real pleasure in watching your dog work.

In the end, of course, this strategy is a tool. It helps you find flocks, but only if you are a serious turkey hunter yourself. You need to hunt your canine where you'll likely locate birds. You need to scout and piece the puzzle together, as always. A turkey dog is only as effective as its handler.

The inclusion of dogs as a hunting option by modern wildlife managers is based on different perspectives. States such as Vermont permit the strategy as a byproduct of upland bird hunting (namely for grouse and woodcock), and this is true for other autumn locations where the approach is permitted. Since wild turkey season is also underway at the same time in some of these states, dogs are legal. On the other hand, places like Virginia and West Virginia have a long-standing tradition of fall turkey dogging, as does New York, where folks like Turkey Trot Acres's Pete Clare employ the strategy as part of their commercial hunting operations using Byrne turkey dogs.

FINDING A TURKEY DOG

So you want a turkey dog, eh? English setters and pointers (especially those that won't hold point), Labrador retrievers, hounds such as hard-running beagles, Brittany spaniels, and even mixed breeds are capable of becoming decent turkey dogs, again, assuming you take the time to hunt that dog where it'll find flocks.

Boykin spaniels were bred historically in the Carolinas for turkey dogging, though ironically South Carolina offers no modern fall season, and North Carolina provides only a winter option. Still, this breed is used in other parts of the country where the tactic is legal and is particularly effective in smaller woodlots where this short-legged canine can find and flush flocks.

English setters and pointers (especially those that won't hold point), Labrador retrievers, hounds such as hard-running beagles, Brittany spaniels, and even mixed breeds are capable of becoming decent turkey dogs—again, assuming you take the time to hunt that dog where it'll find flocks.

Developed by John Byrne and his son J. T. of Lowry, Virginia (pictured here), Appalachian turkey dogs are pointer/setter/Plott-hound crosses bred specifically for fall turkey hunting. These canines are part of an established line intended to maintain an ongoing tradition.

Mine are English setters bred to hunt grouse and woodcock. Midge—the best flock finder in the house—is a wide-ranging bird dog, which is a no-no for ruffs and timberdoodles, but desirable for fall turkeys. Our longtime relationship seems fated: a turkey hunter who owns a like-minded bird dog. A dog that refuses to hold steady on scented upland game, but instead flushes birds, might be a perfect match for you, too.

Sometimes the intention is more deliberate. Developed by John Byrne and his son J. T. of Lowry, Virginia, Appalachian turkey dogs are pointer/setter/Plott-hound crosses bred specifically for fall turkey hunting. These canines are part of an established line intended to maintain an ongoing tradition. Apart from this willful breeding effort, turkey hunters can still chance at finding a cast-off dog that possesses the nose to find flocks and the desire to flush them.

In the end, what do you want? Ideally, a turkey dog should cast ahead, check back to your position, and find flocks. Sometimes turkeys are still tough to find, with or without the dog's help. When it locates

After the flush, the dog should consent to blind time. Concealed in a camouflage bag or behind blind material or both, the dog should rest calmly as turkeys approach your position. Here Pat Brennan sets up with turkey dog Sky.

birds—either by foot, airborne scent, visual contact, or all three—the dog should run at the birds, bark to declare the flock's position, then chase down singles and lingering turkeys into the air. After the flush, the dog should consent to blind time. Concealed in a camouflage bag or behind blind material or both, the dog should rest calmly as turkeys approach your position.

Sometimes your dog will doze off until your shot arouses it. Other times it will lift its head on hearing far-off turkeys before you do. Using a dog to hunt wild turkeys is never a surefire deal. Trying to hide the dog in the blind from the wary eyes of regrouping turkeys sometimes offsets the flushing advantage. That's part of the challenge.

IS A TURKEY DOG RIGHT FOR YOU?

In my mind, the practice of busting flocks and bagging dogs—along with the lengthy off-season that includes all those other intangible pleasures such as training, conditioning, and just plain napping on the couch with one of them—involves a high level of moral and ethical commitment.

In my mind, turkey dogging—along with the lengthy off-season that includes all those other intangible pleasures such as training, conditioning, and just plain napping on the couch with one of your canine buds—involves a high level of moral and ethical commitment.

Training a turkey dog—or any bird-finding canine, for that matter— is based on two things: showing the dog what you want it to do, and reading that animal's natural abilities for what it might offer in the field. The marriage of these two components makes for a reliable hunting partner.

Are you a serious fall and winter turkey hunter? Do you live in or near a state that permits the strategy? Do you have locations where you can condition and train your dog in the off-season? To use your dog as a tool during the hunting season, you have to spend the rest of the year training it. You have to know how to use its abilities in the field. Or at least you should.

Ask yourself: are you truly a dog person, or just one who wants to use that animal during the season, while the rest of the time it sits looking at you from behind the locked gate of an outdoor kennel? You owe that canine hunting partner more than just part-time attention.

Some guys say that keeping a bird dog indoors spoils that canine and makes it a poor hunter. It's one of the most ridiculous statements I've ever heard. It's self-serving and ignorant and should go the way of similarly outdated theories such as the earth is flat, and bloodletting cures illness.

As I write this, one of our English setters, Midge—whose tenth season of turkey dogging approaches—naps on the floor to my right, eyeing me now and again on the off-chance I slip into my boots and indicate we're going outdoors. Half-sister to Midge, old girl Jenny's telltale whistling wheeze tells me she's napping on the dog bed behind me. Another, our boy setter Radar and cousin to the other two, softly snores in his large, open dog crate to my left. We have a deep bond, these dogs and I. As their pack leader when afield, I'm connected to them, and they pay attention to my every move. My life as a dog man reflects this commitment, love, and desire. Yours should, too.

Yes, maybe I'm a little too hard on those who think that a turkey dog will solve all their hunting problems without any investment of time. I've met several guys like that, and those encounters have stuck with me. Those who consider themselves turkey doggers rank all other outdoor activities as second best. For us, this is the real deal. It's a lifestyle.

Do you not mind the smell of a wet gun dog covered with burrs that'll need tending to that night? Do you enjoy walking as much as shooting? Do you smile on seeing your canine find and flush wild turkeys into the air? Do you like the hunt as much as the kill? If so, there's hope for you.

My sense of training dogs first involved my dad's rabbit-hounding beagles—a twenty-five-year experience that involved pre-season runs and in-season hunts. To this day, that's a fond and lasting memory from my childhood. That initial foundation meant everything to me as a teenager and is responsible for my development as an adult dog man.

Jenny, my super-smart canine that's more catlike than some felines, relies more on visual recognition of turkeys before she sprints in and greets the flock in her playful, cheetah-fast style. On her first flock break ever, she kept returning to a tractor trail on the perimeter of a piney woods, sniffing the turkey scent there—though I had no idea of that, as no visual sign suggested it. When she boogied into the woods, I heard alarm putting and witnessed a big flock flushing through the tall white pines.

Midge, my hard-driving, big-hearted, self-hunting, just-this-side-of-wild canine, got into turkeys early in her life and liked it. To me, she's the model of a turkey dog. She casts ahead, checks back (usually), is bag-and-blind trained, barks on the flush (a bonus), and will forever be the dog that allowed me to bridge the understanding of turkey dogging to actual practice in the field. She is responsible for many of my memorable Vermont and New York State autumn turkeys, including those birds tagged on hunts with other gunners. Her list includes autumn longbeards, super jakes, and jakes-of-the-year, plus adult and juvenile hens. There are those memorable birds that eluded us, too.

Enter my Radar, boy setter, who is closer to the traditional New England grouse and woodcock dog he and his two cousins were bred to be. Yes, he moves wild turkeys, but generally only after he's pointed them. On such occasions, these big birds will suddenly act like pheasants and break into long-legged runs. He follows, since none of my dogs are trained to be steady to wing. You haven't experienced the true meaning of a flock flush until you've seen a wad of wild turkeys explode skyward just off a tri-colored English setter's nose. How turkeys can hide in a field of frosted goldenrod before flushing I'll never know.

No matter how your gun dog represents its interest in turkey flocks, you can use it as a tool—assuming, of course, you're a turkey hunter, too.

PUPPY SCHOOL

I believe bird dogs, including those you use to hunt turkeys, are better trained indoors where that bond is consistent and outdoors where you reinforce hunting style. Daily opportunities for training include basic verbal commands and the steadily implied sense that you are in charge—a loving but pack-leading human they likely view as one tall dog that stands on two legs instead of four. Companionship is essential. Spend time with your pup from the moment you bring it home. Start the learning process immediately. Teach commands during feeding times. Have fun with them as they learn.

Introduce your pup to the crate on the first day that dog comes home. If your canine associates the positives of going afield with kenneling up in your vehicle, training and travel will surely run more smoothly.

Outdoors, you want your dog to work ahead, check back, and move through cover using its instincts to find birds. To do so, regular time afield is required. Verbal commands include the usual array of phrases—the simpler, the better. Whistles can be used in association with commands. Hand signals paired with your body movements will have your dog paying attention to the way you move through habitats. Learning comes from repetition. It's important to select the basics you'll use from the first day together throughout the dog's life.

Teach "kennel up" to get your canine to vault into the dog box for transport to hunting and training locales. Introduce your pup to the crate on the first day that dog comes home. Kennel that dog on local trips to condition and train your canine partner, and do so on road trips to turkey-dogging states. If your dog associates the positives of going afield with kenneling up in the back of your vehicle, training and travel will surely run more smoothly.

Use "come," "sit," stay," and "whoa" to do the obvious. I often pair the dog's name with the word, as in "Jenny, come." Choose a simple name, and use it to teach that dog English as its second language. Continue this training the rest of the dog's life. There are plenty of good books, publications, videos, and DVDs on the subject of dog training. Combine the training skills shared there with your knowledge of fall and winter turkey hunting, and you'll do fine. Make training sessions fun. Develop those skill sets in your dog (and yourself), so that year-round training is as enjoyable as hunts. Whatever you do, don't break the dog's spirit.

There are many theories on introducing your pup to the gun. If possible, do so when the dog is engaged in the hunt, ideally during the fall turkey season. My dogs associate a shotgun's report with the potential of finding game, and that's good. After a gunshot from our blind setup, Midge routinely scrambles to find the downed turkey in front of our location. In a sense, that's her reward—and, of course, mine.

How do you hide the dog? A blind helps. A bag offers backup support. John Byrne, who came up with this idea originally, carries zippered camouflage cloth bags made by his wife for this purpose. In fact, the concealment bag is now widespread throughout the turkey dogging subculture, as many of us have employed various versions of this original notion.

I have two bags, both designed by my wife. One is of thin camo material with a sturdy zipper, which I use on warm early-season autumn hunts. The other—made of a thicker leaf-patterned fabric with an insulated fleece lining inside—comes with us when cold winds blow and snow flies. But first you have to get the dog comfortable with being slipped inside the bag. If they fight that, you're finished.

My Midge is so accustomed to the bag in the field that following a flush she quite nearly climbs into it at the setup site. I slip her into concealing camouflage, with her head peeking out, zipper gently drawn around her neck.

To bag train your pup, start young—eight weeks of age is about right. First get the dog comfortable sitting on your lap, or curled up in front of you for periods of time. This can be done while watching television or even reading this book during the off-season. During the season, you can take the dog afield and apply that training in the outdoors. If it's legal in your state, you can obviously do so in the off-season as well.

My Midge is so accustomed to the bag in the field that following a flush she quite nearly climbs into it at the setup site. I slip her into the bag, with her head peeking out, zipper gently drawn around her neck. To seal the deal, I use a roll-up camo blind around my setup for added insurance against the wary eyes of wild turkeys. Sometimes she dozes off. Sometimes she's on steady alert. I may have to calm her as turkeys approach.

Pointing dogs are bred to scent, then point the nearby presence of gamebirds, holding their statuesque poses until the armed gunner steps up and flushes that quarry. Additionally, handlers of such canines routinely train pups to hold point when that winged game takes to the air. To develop a turkey dog from a pointing breed, introduce them to the birds you want them to hunt, but hold off on finishing them to hold steady to wing and shot.

Why? Often turkeys will break and run on noting the presence of a dog, and you want your canine hunting buddy to pursue them and get them into the air. My Radar scents the big birds the same way he does grouse—even pointing tight-holding turkey flocks when we encounter them—but he runs at the group when they begin to move off on foot or if some take wing, leaving others behind.

Owners of flushing breeds need only to train their dogs to hunt based on their commands, knowing that once the desired game is found (turkeys in this case), such dogs will make those flocked-up birds take wing. Hounds, often renegades by design, will also track and move turkey flocks.

Granted, some breeds will hunt closer than others. I've known of Boykin spaniels and Brittanys that are surefire turkey finders in smaller woodlots, while renegade English setters like my Midge run big, and are best used in expansive agricultural settings and on rolling ridge tops and broad hillsides.

DOGGING GEAR

Vest: Since dogging turkeys is a strictly autumn and winter option, the following necessities will add weight to your vest. Think pockets, and plenty of them. You need places to put all your gear and dog accessories. Padded shoulder straps will help you lug extra weight through turkey country. Decent seat cushions—which often come with modern turkey vest options—are a must as well.

Collapsible water bowl: I carry these afield year-round and train my dogs to check back for thirst-quenching pit stops. This helps minimize their attempts to drink from questionable water sources and keeps them hydrated. Water bottles fit nicely inside these bowls, which can be carried in the back of your field vest, or inside a camouflaged fanny pack. Many are made of durable polyester cloth with leak-proof nylon linings, and double as feeding bowls.

Camouflage blinds: I carry leaf-patterned burlap material that rolls up tightly and sits nestled in the bottom of my game vest until I need it for setups. Deadfall and branches always seem to be readily available in the woods to provide a frame for the fabric, which I drape over that natural cover. I've also had success with portable blinds that can be carried in the back of my vest.

Since the early 1990s I've written about turkey dogging for print publications, been part of filmed dog hunts for television, and talked about it on the radio. I've fielded questions on the phone and via email from guys who are just starting out. I've taken hunters with me to introduce them to the sport. I enjoy it. It's what I do. It's all good.

A vet's first-aid kit: Put whatever you can inside this, in no particular order: a pocket knife, tweezers, dog nail trimmers, antibiotic ointment, artificial tears (to remove foreign eye particles), hydrogen peroxide, a space blanket, a pen light (it always eventually gets dark, at least where I hunt), an absorbent cotton roll, ace bandages, adhesive tape, and anything else you can think of, including a multi-tool for possible heavy-duty porcupine encounters. Ideally, you'd keep all this in a waterproof container.

Miscellaneous dog accessories: This list would include a sturdy lead, extra collar, and blaze-orange dog vest for use in heavily hunted areas when seasons overlap (remove the latter item at your setup). I even occasionally run bells on collars to alert hunters of our presence and to help me track dogs. Ironically, the inherent noise doesn't seem to affect our ability to find and flush turkeys at all. Carry a snack for you and your dog as well. A gun sling for your firearm is another essential to help you lug your load. You'll want a grooming brush for downtime in camp. Um, for your dog, that is.

DOGGING NETWORK

Since the early 1990s I've written about turkey dogging for print publications, been part of filmed dog hunts for television, and talked about it on the radio. I've fielded questions on the phone and via email from guys who are just starting out. I've taken hunters with me to introduce them to the sport. I enjoy it. It's what I do. It's all good.

To learn the tradition, spend time with those who do it. Ask questions. True enough, there are some dog men who prefer to hunt privately on their own (I resist calling them a secret society because that's a bit too strong of a phrase), but most guys who practice this like talking about their dogs and hunts.

THE WINGSHOOTING QUESTION

Typically turkey dogs are used as a tool to find and flush autumn and winter flocks, so you might call turkeys back more effectively. Situations occur where it might even be warranted to take a gobbler or hen on the flush. Should you? Sometimes, yes. Often, no. Competent wingshooters can drop birds, especially young-of-year turkeys. A friend took such a bird on the wing right after Midge flushed it. That young-of-the-year hen dropped like a sack of laundry. Be honest with your abilities, though. Shoot for the head, not the body, just as you would if the turkey stood on the ground in range.

It's also important to know the dog's location just as you would double-check the position of a human hunting partner, as accidents can happen. Your dog might be right behind a single turkey on the ground, moving in fast pursuit. I've seen this many times. Another hunting buddy—a safe and reliable shooter if ever—once passed on pulling the trigger during two different New York hunts when my Midge moved too closely behind flushing adult fall gobblers in gun range. If that's not a test of will and sensibility, I don't know what is. As if rewarded for his mental toughness, he eventually called in and killed a Vermont autumn long-beard from a gang of birds Midge had found and flushed.

Safety is an issue. Pick the guys you hunt with wisely. That's not always an option, though. As a result, some turkey doggers don't load their guns until they're set up in the blind after the flush. In truth, the essence of fall dogging involves flushing flocks, setting up in a concealed hide, and then calling the turkeys back to your setup.

On selective hunts, I've seen buddies take flushing turkeys on the wing, while others have employed strict discipline when facing the prospect of making a shot at a departing gobbler or hen that's too close to the dog. All get my admiration and respect, depending on the specific hunting situation. Safety and common sense rule.

GAME TIME

Those who do it know it. Those who don't, sometimes puzzle over the strategy. I once dogged wild turkeys with a bird-hunting traditionalist and gun dog guy who was accustomed to stylish canines that would find grouse and woodcock, then point them with staunch poses. Enter Midge.

Turkey dogs need to exhibit a hard-driving, bird-crazy desire to find and flush autumn flocks.

As my wild-child English setter flash-pointed woodcock, then Eastern cottontails, then ruffed grouse in succession (this was a game-rich habitat, if ever)—with me ignoring them all—he turned and said, "I can't understand why you don't have the desire to make her into a pure pointing dog." I grinned.

Later that day my renegade pointing dog flushed a monster flock of turkeys—one of which we killed after several exciting peaks and valleys during the post-flush, call-back session. His own grin held an answer to his question.

Running your dog alone ensures a somewhat predictable range of expectations for your turkey hunt. Introducing your dog into a situation where other unfamiliar canines are hunting at the same time can change the matter entirely.

Some want to play. Some want to fight. Some male dogs want to romance females, while some hunt-minded bitches could care less about such distracted suitors. Such interactions and dynamics should always be considered. If the dogs have hunted together before, you might not have that much of a challenge. The truth is, I don't think human handlers can ever entirely predict how new dogs will act together.

Carrying gear for both you and your dog will add weight to your vest—especially if you go afield with more than one canine, as does Turkey Trot Acres's Pete Clare.

On one fall hunt, I ran my setter Midge with a brawny, turkey-minded, uncastrated male dog of mixed lineage. Seconds into the hunt, my normally calm and collected female tore into him, asserting her dominance. Fortunately, his handler understood dog language and we agreed not to hunt them together again during that road trip.

On another fall hunt, Midge was paired with the late-great Kelly—the first Byrne turkey dog I ever hunted with. Forget that they looked like identical twins. I'd always held a fondness for Pete Clare's Kelly dog, so when she turned, growled, and rolled my sweetheart Midge, I was a little more forgiving than in another situation.

Why persist at putting dogs together? Why not always hunt them apart? Truth is, on road trips with many turkey dogs along, each guy wants to run his. Time is limited. Several dogs can increase your chances of finding flocks, and sometimes unfamiliar combinations do work.

The October turkey hunt wasn't going well at first. Two male dogs were literally hounding my lemon-and-white setter girl, sniffing, prodding, and generally annoying her. Even though she's spayed, they were still-intact boys being boys. Midge acted like she wanted to climb into the back of my turkey vest. Something had to be done.

Miscellaneous gear items include a sturdy lead, extra collar, and blaze-orange dog vest for use in heavily hunted areas when seasons overlap.

Pat Brennan, a longtime guide out of Clare's Turkey Trot Acres, suggested that we hunt Midge with another female named Sky, who I'd hunted with as a pup, and who had had a reputation for being strong-willed and selective about her dogging partners. Amazingly, they acted like old friends, hunting well together, and eventually finding a turkey flock. It's just a theory founded on human speculation, but all I can say is that Midge looks like Kelly, one of Sky's running mates, while Sky looks like my tri-colored Jenny, Midge's half-sister. Though of course dogs note each other by scent and gesture, too, whatever accounted for the perfect combination doesn't matter. It worked.

TRUST

I wanted to go up the trail to the top of the Vermont mountain, since that's the direction fresh turkey droppings were leading. Plus, to my human legs and mind, it was the path of least resistance. "Midgey, come," I flatly demanded, but she ignored the command, moved west and away from me, up a hilly rise. Hmm. I glanced in that direction to see fresh scratchings beneath ground cover—sign I would have missed otherwise. Soon I heard my dog barking, and several turkeys winged overhead to confirm what she'd found, while alarm putting continued in earshot, but just out of sight. A little over an hour later, we were coming down the trail with a tagged turkey in the back of my vest. I'd still be walking had I not trusted her.

Lawrence Pyne and Steve Hickoff's English setter Midge sit with two Vermont autumn turkeys taken by the author and Pyne on a Halloween hunt.

Make that dog your buddy, and take her everywhere you can from day one. This is how the bond is forged.

END GAME

In the end, it's pretty simple:

- To become a serious fall turkey dogger, read all you can on the history of the tradition and of ways to train your dog to hunt with you.
- Realize you are first hunting for your dog, and then for yourself.
- Consider some of your success as being measured in flock finds and flushes.
- Make that dog your buddy, and take her everywhere you can from day one. This is how the bond is forged.
- Hunt where the strategy is legal and develop friendships with turkey doggers who are serious about the tradition.
- After you've done everything possible to train that animal, trust your dog. Turkey dogging is a combination of your hunting experiences and your canine's ability to find flocks.
- Get out, get out, whenever you can.

Running your dog alone ensures a somewhat predictable range of expectations for your turkey hunt. Introducing your dog into a situation where other unfamiliar canines are hunting at the same time can change the matter entirely.

Most of the time you want your turkey dog to move ahead of you to find and flush turkeys. But sometimes you can use a lead to control when your dog flushes flocks you've seen and gain an advantage over those turkeys.

A time to hunt; a time to rest.

CHAPTER 14

The camouflage you wear during your spring hunts will also work fine for your woodstove-month outings. Those fall and winter turkey hunters who wish to bolster their confidence even more will find season-specific and terrain-related patterns for open expanses or wooded areas available.

Gearing Up

Performance. Reliability. Ease of use. Comfort. This lead sounds like an advertorial, but that's what you need in gear. First, you have to hide.

BECOMING A TREE

The camouflage you wear during your spring hunts will also work fine for your woodstove-month outings. Those fall and winter turkey hunters who wish to bolster their confidence even more will find season-specific as well as terrain-related patterns for open expanses or wooded areas available. Since camouflage companies license their images to clothing manufacturers, quality in product can vary widely, from simple to technically detailed.

I'm old enough to remember a time when there was no camouflage other than standard military issue. As the son of a turkey hunter, I grew up watching my dad first spray paint a putty-colored suit with splashes of bark-red and pine-green to create a kind of primitive camouflage that actually fooled a number of memorable gobblers. You see, he grew up a Pennsylvania fall turkey hunter, well before the spring season was legalized in the late 1960s. That shift in tradition changed everything—for the Keystone State and the rest of the turkey hunting world.

Enter the outdoor industry's camouflage in its many visual flavors. I did all of my autumn turkey hunting as a Pennsylvania teenager wearing standard hunting boots, old blue jeans, and a sand-drab field jacket with a pumpkin-orange cap on top of my head. But things changed by the time I passed thirty and began turkey hunting in northern New England and New York State.

New ways to hide were evolving. But first, I reflexively did what any self-respecting, I-don't-really-know-what's-in-style, late-1980s turkey hunter would have done: I went to an Army-Navy store. Fully expecting

Before modern camouflage evolved to today's standards, turkey hunters mixed and matched military camouflage with early outdoor-industry patterns.

to purchase some of the standard issue stuff at a discount, I was more than pleased when I saw a variety of items on the rack that seemed to indicate an emerging camouflage trend first evidenced in several of the turkey magazines at the time. Bib overalls and step-in jumpsuits. Face masks instead of paint.

Back then I didn't have closets full of each and every option as I do now, apparel in Realtree, Advantage, Mossy Oak, Skyline, and Natural Gear patterns. These days I mix. I match. When particular hunts stay lucky during a string of outings, I stick with the combinations. And I can't throw that old stuff away, either—too many good memories there. Besides, I flat-out love camo. I feel more comfortable and more like myself when I'm suited up in one of the leaf-pattern options. There's a certain nostalgia involved. Maybe I like the fact that head to toe it makes me look like a bearded face on a 6-foot, 2-inch tree. I think a lot of guys are like this—those that like to rise earlier than later and chase these birds with a shared passion. You blend in. . . .

While some non-hunters might routinely wonder why you can't fill particular turkey tags each year, what with the fact the visible flocks sometimes just stand alongside major interstates as traffic zips past, the rest of us know that wild turkeys in big pasture fields and mountain ridge tops don't act like that. You have to hide.

Wild turkeys run when you just think of them. That's why you wear camo. That's why you have to blend in to have just a semblance of a chance. You have to cover your head with leaf-patterned ball caps on warm late-afternoon October hunts, and with drawstring hoods on chilly winter daybreaks. You have wear space-age underwear that makes you and your buddies look like phantasmagorical ballet dancers in the early hours at turkey camps around the country. You have to step into pants with many pockets, and shirts with many pockets, and vests with many more pockets, and all of it camouflaged. Fully committed to the tradition, you have no choice. Heck, they even make leaf-patterned toilet paper to lend confidence when nature calls.

Forget that I once called in a New Hampshire gobbler gang with swinging beards while bowhunting turkeys during the also-open deer firearms season, and that I not only wore camouflaged pants and a mesh face mask, but also a blaze-orange hooded sweatshirt. I was half-dressed for concealed confidence from turkeys, and half-dressed for conspicuous-

Wild turkeys run when you just think of them. That's why you wear camo. That's why you have to blend in to have just a semblance of a chance.

It's important for a turkey hunter to cover his face. In truth, if you mount your gun before the turkey arrives in full view, chances are your mug will be concealed as you look down the barrel. Still, wild turkeys can creep in unexpectedly.

ness for whitetail hunters, I guess, sitting there against a maple tree. I gobbler-yelped to autumn toms I had scattered the night before. In time, they got together, then eased in to ten nearby steps, and I drew my arrow without being seen. Well, you know bowhunting, especially the kind done without the help of a concealing portable blind, which I should have had. Anyhow, I clattered a broadhead-tipped shaft off branchy deadfall in front of the nearest gobbler. They surely spooked then.

While my stick-and-string abilities can be questioned, calling up adult fall gobblers while looking like some orange-and-camo clad highway worker is a measure of certain accomplishment. In the end, camouflage is there for when certain backcountry birds threaten to run on seeing your heart beating beneath leafy fabric. It's there for when you cough as that turkey steps into view. It's there for when you fall asleep, then wake up as a flock of a dozen fall turkeys crunches by in gun range. Camouflage makes you feel like you're actually part of the woods, and I have to believe it fools wildlife.

I was on downtime in Texas one year, hunting turkeys but taking a little break. It was late morning. The sun felt good the way the Lone Star State sun should when you've just taken three flights from icy New

England to get to west Texas. I saw a mama squirrel and her young moving toward me, my camouflage allowing me to blend into the surroundings like just another slumping length of deadfall.

In succession, one squirrel after another, each furry animal stepped up on my right snake boot's toe (also camouflaged), and then walk-hopped my full length to my head. Each sat there for a second or two atop my hat, then jumped off and climbed up the actual tree. It was nothing less than amazing as all followed from toe to knee to chest to head, and then up and up. I could hear them scratching bark above me with their claws as they ascended. After more than three decades of trying to hide in the woods, I had finally become a tree.

VESTED INTERESTS

Gear. The final frontier. You can never have enough of it. I don't know of any outdoor sporting pursuit that requires as much as turkey hunting, except maybe fly fishing, where a many-pocketed vest is also involved.

As mentioned, turkey dogging gear—again, a decidedly fall and winter feature—will increase your vest's weight. Dogless, you can travel lighter, or simply load yourself down with a calling and survival-mode arsenal. Your turkey vest's pockets carry the weight of your gear and your hopes for success. Your tools for that day's hunt might be simple or complicated by choice, no matter what the season. Turkey hunting is turkey hunting, period.

A hunting bud asked me recently, so I told him: a dozen or so turkey vests hang in my closets—others are semi-retired in plastic bins. That's not counting the shirts, pants, and jackets that also have enough pockets to qualify as vests.

As modern turkey vests go, most have fair to superb organizational features; that's why you have so many—even if it takes a while to learn where you've stored stuff early in the season. They have box call pockets, with built-in call silencers. They have places for your slates and strikers, your mouth call cases, your many other accessories, and even your lunch. Some have attached seat cushions, padded backs, and elaborate fold-down, well-supported, chair-like seats. I own a range of light vests for warm days, and heavy vests with padded shoulder straps for lugging gear, and vests for cold-weather hunts. Some vests even have detachable sleeves. And every now and again I discover a pocket I hadn't even known about.

In autumn and winter, you won't need a crow call or owl hooter to locate gobblers (unless you want to make non-verbal contact with a hunting buddy that way; if not, there's an extra pocket to use), but many other turkey hunting tools remain the same. At some point, you'll likely need the following items, some of which can be left home given the time of the season and demands of the hunting situation, and others which definitely need to be in your vest of choice.

A flashlight: You won't need it often, and it should be used sparingly, but this tool is occasionally necessary for creeping along in the dark toward roosted fall and winter turkeys—especially if you get in there real early. A flashlight, or a smaller, sleeker penlight which fits in a vest pocket, can help you when leaving the woods after darkness falls. Always flash it off and on at the ground as you walk and never skyward into the trees. On a full moon autumn night, you may not even need it. On new moon evenings, with overcast skies, you surely will.

Sunglasses: A no-brainer, right? But if you forget sunglasses and find yourself sitting on a field edge for patterned autumn turkeys during a bright sunny day without them, you'll be cursing yourself. Just make sure you can comfortably mount your gun or draw your bow at that moment of truth.

A mesh facemask: It's important for a turkey hunter to cover that face. In truth, if you mount your gun before the turkey arrives in full view, chances are your mug will be concealed as you look down the barrel. Still, wild turkeys can creep in unexpectedly. Camouflaged facemasks conceal you in the event you're caught off-guard. Masks give you confidence you're hidden. I'm convinced that when approaching a field for a look-see, wearing a bandito-style facemask is better than having it down around your neck.

Camouflaged gloves: You can kill a turkey without them, sure, but wearing gloves gives you a certain confidence as well. Some with gripper dots on the palms can afford you better gun-mounting ability—helpful on showery fall hunts. On winter days, gloves are nearly essential. If you're uncomfortable with the feel of your trigger finger covered with fabric, simply snip off material to expose that crucial digit. (Um, make sure you take the glove off first.)

Roll-up raingear: Some might argue that you still get wet donning raingear, but roll-up, wet-weather jackets offer you another windbreaker to wear. One can fit snugly at the bottom of your game bag, with or without a turkey in there. (I own about a dozen of these, too.)

Midmorning snack: Not such a big deal as you slip out of the house or camp before daybreak, your adrenal glands firing on all cylinders, but by midmorning you'll be wishing you'd stashed a treat away. Two schools of thought rule here: some guys like to take their breakfast at local diners (where they might get both a hot meal and recent word of a farmer's turkey flock), while others like to stay in the woods as much as possible.

You can kill a turkey without them, sure, but wearing camouflage gloves gives you a certain confidence. Some with gripper dots on the palms can afford you better gun-mounting ability—helpful on showery fall hunts. On winter days, gloves are nearly essential.

At any rate, energy bars (the kind M. D. Johnson jokes about in the foreword) travel well and offer quick fixes. Bottled water is my number one choice of beverage. I often stash an apple or banana in there, too, to get me by. Trail mix. Check. Candy bars. Check. Gum, mints, or even your favorite smokeless tobacco can slake hunger, if only to give your mouth something to do other than working a diaphragm. It's your call, but carry something in there. If it's highly portable beef jerky—delicious but thirst-provoking—stash an extra water bottle.

A pocket knife: Make mine lightweight with a sharp cutting edge for gutting and later cutting breast fillets and other bird parts. Use that knife to check the bird's crop contents as well, which will help you determine what that particular turkey was feeding on that day. I personally think you should use as much of the edible meat on a wild turkey as possible, so game snips—kept back at camp—will aid this process as well.

Pruning shears: Use these to fashion openings for your field-edge setups, and to cut branches from deadfall for post-break call-back sessions in the woods. Clear shooting lanes. Get landowner permission if you're

Make my hunting knife lightweight with a sharp cutting edge for gutting the turkey and later cutting breast fillets and other bird parts. Use that knife to check the bird's crop contents as well, which will help you determine what that particular turkey was feeding on that day.

not on public property. Check local laws to see if permanent blinds and the snipping of tree limbs are legal in your area.

Binoculars: Your eagle eyes may have faded some as you've aged, and binoculars can help. As with pruning shears, this tool is sometimes cumbersome to carry, but certain times—such as long-distance flock identification—dictate that you need them. You can glass open fields, hilly hollows, ridge tops, and creek bottoms from a distance. Before leaf drop, you may have to get in the woods to view flocks. After the leaves fall, you can often see groups of turkeys feeding along hillsides. This is especially true in winter when dark moving blobs gleam with shiny-black sunstruck backs while walking over recent snow. As a tactic, glassing birds can help you determine the direction they're moving in.

If it's early morning, their roost might not be far away. If it's midday, they might loaf there on a regular basis, dusting and sunning between active feeding times. If it's mid to late afternoon, you can watch the

Your eagle eyes may have faded some as you've aged, and binoculars can help when glassing fields. This tool is sometimes cumbersome to carry, but certain times—such as long-distance flock identification—dictate that you need them.

direction they're heading to fix that roosting location for the following morning's hunt. Using binoculars can also help you determine the sex of birds.

Many states offer fall and winter hunts for either-sex turkeys, where all kinds of birds—juvenile or adult—are legal. Still, identifying the sex of birds using optics can allow you to determine how you'll call in the woods. Put simply, it can also help you confirm that those blobs are actually turkeys, and not dark windblown bushes.

Certain binocular-obsessed hunters raise their optical aids as turkeys come into view at fairly close range. More than once I've seen birds go suspicious and move off at this tactical error. If a flock is that close, call them in closer, and see what sex they are with the naked eye.

A camera: Hero shots are always better when taken where you tagged the turkey, because the land you hunt is often as memorable as the bird you took there. A small tripod, with a working know-how of how to

When hunting a new area, you can study topographical maps, fold several into a plastic bag, and stash them in your vest for use during your time afield.

set a self-timer, can be carried if you hunt alone, or if you and your buddy want to pose in the same grip-and-grin image. More stuff to lug, yes, but you'll have that memory.

Maps: Internet sites provide geographical references, and standard print maps also work fine. When hunting a new area, you can photocopy topographical maps, fold several into a plastic bag, and stash them in your vest. Others simply fire up their global positioning systems to get a location fix. Mental notes of specific landmarks and compass readings can help you map your way as well.

Change of socks: You cover territory with your booted feet, so why not stay as comfortable as possible. Carry several pairs. Stay away from 100 percent cotton, as such material doesn't wick away moisture. Many of the wool, polypropylene, nylon, and Lycra blends do, while simultaneously keeping your feet warm—a must on fall and winter turkey hunts. Yes, I sometimes even carry a spare pair in my vest. Overindulgent? Hey, they're my size-12 feet!

Insect spray: Depending on where you live, early-season fall hunts might require you to carry a small bottle of repellent afield. The list of crawling and flying bugs that bite demands it—unless you simply tough it out.

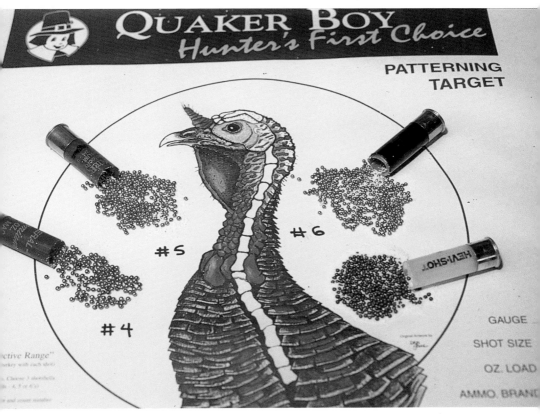

In truth, you only need one shell for a single deliberate shot, but things happen. There are lots of options out there for you to test pattern.

Magnum shotgun shells: In truth, you only need one shell for a single deliberate shot if a one-bird fall/winter limit is in place, but things happen. Carry several to a half-dozen loads—buddies might occasionally need a loaner (matching proper shell to gun, of course)—just to be ready. If you only had one shell to carry in your vest, you'd ensure the shot was good, right? There's no harm in aspiring to that high standard, of course, no matter how many shells you tote in your vest. Make that trigger pull count.

Turkey calls: You may own several to several hundred options here. Bare minimum, you'll need a double-reed mouth diaphragm (to kee-kee and kee-kee-run during family flock encounters), a slate, glass, or aluminum pot-and-peg call (to make hen and gobbler yelps), and a versatile box call because no turkey hunter—fall, winter, or spring—should be

In many autumn and winter states, it's legal to take a turkey of either sex, so as ever, safety rules when using decoys—even more so than in spring when gobblers are the aim.

caught in the woods without one. Modern vests provide pockets for all three options, and zippered storage pouches, plastic hole-ventilated carriers, and plastic bags can assist you further. Carry chalk to tune box calls (though some require no chalking), and light-grit sandpaper to dress slates. Striker tips can be gently sanded with emery.

Decoys: No matter the season, fake turkeys can help draw a bird into gun or bow range and right into the shooting lane you've chosen. Wild turkey hunters (many of whom are also waterfowlers at heart) can set big spreads of a half-dozen or more foam birds in a field to imitate a fall or winter flock. Where legal, modern dekes offer remote-control motion to create realism. In many states, it's legal to take a turkey of either sex, so as ever, safety rules when using decoys—even more so than in spring when gobblers are the aim. You may lure in more than just birds.

Many turkey hunters—primarily spring enthusiasts—use decoys to tag breed-driven gobblers. On the other hand, foam fakes also can limit mobility once staked in the ground. Now and again, decoys even frighten turkeys that come into view just out of range. Sometimes you assume it's a pecking-order issue if a young fall gobbler sees a jake deke and decides to back off. Other times, it's the lack of realism in an unmoving decoy that might do it. Sometimes turkeys simply seem to ignore them.

Blinds: Establishing camouflage blinds along travel routes to and from fall and winter turkey roosts to feeding zones allows you to come and go any time of the day. Most blinds are both portable and sturdy. Once concealed inside, shooting windows provide views from different directions. Blind material is often weather resistant, which makes it possible to hunt anytime. Often such setups are paired with a comfortable chair inside.

Boots: In early fall, I like non-insulated, waterproof 18-inch rubber boots. Come late autumn, and as winter sets in, I prefer heavy-duty, insulated, waterproof footwear. Swamps, creeks, and streams are a regular feature of seasonal hunts. At times, hip boots you use for trout fishing can help you cross water to the nearby turkey woods. Snake boots are a must in places like Texas, not only for threats of the venomous kind, but also for all the other prickly, thorny vegetation underfoot. Most snakes I've encountered while turkey hunting held their rattling ground or slinked off in a hurry.

TEN BIGGEST GEAR GAFFES

1. Forgetting your seat cushion.
2. Wearing the wrong footwear.
3. Not dressing for the weather.
4. Leaving your wristwatch home.
5. Toting the wrong shotgun load.
6. Not having a backup firearm at camp.
7. Losing your glasses or contacts without a spare pair.
8. Getting lost without a map, compass, or GPS unit.
9. Misplacing your hunting license and turkey permit.
10. Pocketing the wrong calls for the situation.

Dress for the weather. Any questions?

Talk at turkey camp should always include an inventory of gear and a game plan for the day.

CHAPTER 15

Know what your shotgun will do and match it with a load that will do it. The rest is just enjoying the hunt and coaxing the bird into range.

Guns, Loads, Bows, and Broadheads

Our long-suffering spouses endure plenty. When the time comes, I've told my wife Elizabeth I want to be cremated, then reloaded into turkey shotshells. This ammo is to be distributed among my still-living hunting buddies, so that I can keep chasing birds around the country. As a result, the comment "I heard Steve killed two or three this season" might be offered posthumously with a smile at turkey camp somewhere. For now though, there are plenty of less-personalized options on the market.

SHOTSHELLS

Like many of you, I collect turkey memorabilia in an effort to reflect on our tradition. I have a green-and-yellow cardboard box behind glass, now emptied of its 2¾-inch Remington shells, bearing the faded words "Turkey Only" on it, neatly printed there in my father's handwriting.

The 1¼-ounce, 2¾-inch, 16-gauge "Express Magnum" ammo, with a payload of No. 6 shot, was his deliberate choice for use in an Ithaca Model 37 Featherlight slide-action shotgun, back in the days before modern turkey loads evolved—that is, when he wasn't afield with a rifle, legal during the Pennsylvania fall turkey season.

Today we have more options. Still, once you settle on a load that works for you, it's often best to consider sticking with it, even though a range of possible experimentation is also available.

What do you really want from your ammo choice as a wild turkey hunter? In short, a shot pellet transfers energy as a result of velocity and weight. Multiple hits on a turkey's neck and head deliver cumulative energy. Find a load that'll do that for you.

What do you really want from your ammo choice as a wild turkey hunter? In short, a shot pellet transfers energy as a result of velocity and weight. Multiple hits on a turkey's neck and head deliver cumulative energy—a knockdown punch to rival Ali in his prime. The desired results should include a tagged bird and successful completion of the hunt— though the tradition is of course much richer. Find a load that'll do that for you.

I'm lucky. As a working professional and hunting writer, I get to sample many shotgun loads, field-testing these shells around the country during actual hunts, often with a sponsor's firearms shipped in for the occasion. I get to know the loaner tools quickly during the camp's patterning session, then aim to make good during game time on our quarry. It's a crash course from which most of us graduate successfully. Achieving a certain comfort level with a gun and load you've never used before, especially when you tag a bird with it, is that measure of triumph.

It might be professional suicide, or simple unadorned honesty, but every specifically designed turkey shell, choke tube, and firearm I have ever tried on these industry hunts has worked. If turkeys haven't

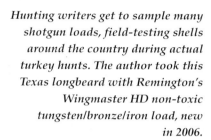

Hunting writers get to sample many shotgun loads, field-testing shells around the country during actual turkey hunts. The author took this Texas longbeard with Remington's Wingmaster HD non-toxic tungsten/bronze/iron load, new in 2006.

dropped, the fault was likely mine. If so, I've usually been to blame for letting the bird get too close, indulging a little too long in those sweet moments as the quarry draws near.

Ideally, a swift, sure kill should take place after the turkey is in range. That's the hunt: getting them close, but not too tight. It starts with pellet size. Number 4s, 5s, and 6s are the standard payload option for wild turkeys and are legal in most states.

As far as my shot size preference goes, I've used many options. As I write this, Winchester Supreme High-Velocity turkey loads remain effective. I'm happy with either No. 5s or 6s in the 3-inch shell length, packing 1³/₄ ounces of shot. I stick with one load personally; I generally hunt with many professionally. Over the last few years of media hunts, I've chambered loads that offer additional long-range capability—a shotshell trend as I write this. Federal, Remington, and Hevi-Shot shells have served me well in the past. All drop turkeys cleanly.

Trust that you don't necessarily have to know why a turkey shotshell works, only that it does when you need it to. To do this, shoot the turkey load through the shotgun and choke tube you want to use. If it's effective

Scattergunning still remains something of an inexact science, especially when you aim and shoot that shotgun like a rifle as you do while turkey hunting. The better you know how your firearm handles a specific load, the more improved are your chances of taking a bird.

at throwing dense patterns at preferred ranges, hunt with that combination. Experiment at the gun range. Make your choice there, and then go afield.

If you are a hunt-by-the-numbers sort of person who likes to dig deep into ballistics data, that's fine. This research might add to your enjoyment of the tradition. This is true for many of my friends, guys who also study their firearms, trucks, and tractors the same way. All major gun industry manufacturers provide this sort of data for their customers, so it's there for your leisurely study. In pre-season armchair mode, it's a pleasure to peruse what's new, even if you fall back on tried-and-true approaches when it counts.

SHOTGUNS

Scattergunning still remains something of an inexact science, especially when you aim and shoot that shotgun like a rifle as you do while turkey hunting. The better you know how your firearm handles a specific load, the more improved are your chances of taking a bird. All that scouting, lost sleep, road miles, plotting, strategizing, calling, and outmaneuvering wild turkeys often comes down to one shot, and that moment of opportunity is often a matter of seconds. You need to be ready.

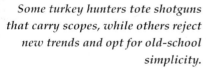

Some turkey hunters tote shotguns that carry scopes, while others reject new trends and opt for old-school simplicity.

Ask yourself: are you interested in calling turkeys so close that your heartbeat is in your throat, or would you prefer to snipe them on the edge of optimum range? Ultimately you decide—as does the wild turkey unknowingly when it presents the opportunity—but your load matched with a suitable shotgun should be up to the task. If you don't have a good shot, don't shoot. When you do, drop that bird dead.

Like every hunter in the turkey woods, spring, fall, or winter, I have my preferences. If I could only go afield with just one shotgun, it would be a Remington 870 pump. Why? Many reasons. It's affordable. It's simple to use and keep in working order. It's versatile, as one of mine allows use of all modern shotshell sizes, while the other two guns handle 2³/₄- and 3-inch loads. Mostly though, it's just comfortable in my arms, and easy to handle. It feels right.

All my turkey hunting buds have their preferences, too, from those whose shotguns are seriously technical and carry scopes, to those who reject new trends and opt for old-school simplicity.

Even one of my timeworn Remington 870 pumps—with its 28-inch, modified-choke barrel, which patterns tightly at 25 yards—has dropped memorable turkeys, doing double-time outside of New England's waterfowling haunts. Go figure. If you aim at the turkey's head and neck, and know what that load, choke, and gun will do, pull the trigger in confidence.

Again, I've handled every kind of big-bore shotgun option that we in the outdoor industry can sample, and scored on wild turkeys. Since you tend to only get one sure poke at a standing bird, a single-shot smoothbore is also undeniably fine, especially for youth hunters who need to think hard on that solitary option.

In truth, my second shots have been few—though a 5-yard miss on a Texas gobbler (too close!) followed by a 47-yard kill (nearly too far!) immediately comes to mind. In my case, I usually miss badly, or anchor cleanly. Buddies joke that "Hickoff likes his turkeys in his lap, and without crap in the way," and that's mostly true, beyond their fun-loving exaggerations. Sure enough, I do try to call birds until they're lured in between 20 to 35 yards away with a clean shooting lane free of most pattern-fragmenting obstructions.

I silently object to long-range kill braggers as they hold forth, though my Lone Star State shot at nearly half a football field makes me a part-time hypocrite. There, the bird popped up way too close, then too far away. I screwed up on the first shot, but time on the patterning range beforehand gave me the assurance the load, choke tube, and gun (at the time one of Big Green's Hevi-Shot loads, and an Extra-Full choke screwed into an 11-87) would deliver a punch at that distance. It did. I'm grateful.

In the fall and winter, you also chance at taking smaller birds-of-the-year, hatch time depending, though young gobblers can stand as tall as their brood hens by then. Smaller gauges that consistently produce tight patterns are deadly on juveniles, too. As mentioned earlier, my dad did most of his turkey shotgunning with a 16-gauge pump. My wife killed her first fall turkey dead with a 20-gauge shellshucker, a bird that folded instantly.

Turkey hunters have varied opinions, and that's good for conversation's sake. Some want to reach out and touch turkeys on the edge of that 40-yard range, and if they know their gun will do that, that's fine. Others are content to draw them in closer. In the end, if you know what the shotgun will do and match it with a load that will do it, the rest is just enjoying the hunt and coaxing the bird into range.

SHOTGUN PATTERNING

Buy a range of turkey loads in No. 4s, 5s, and 6s, and $2^3/4$-, 3-, and $3^1/2$-inch options, shotgun permitting. Share this expense with some friends. Shoot these loads as a form of recreation and study. Figure out which one works best for you and your firearm.

Pattern density matters. Shoot loads at different yardage distances: 10, 20, 30, 40. Density will obviously change. Your maximum distance is determined when fewer pellets fail to hit the head and neck area of that paper target. If that happens at 40 yards, consider only shooting turkeys at a closer maximum distance.

SHOTGUN CHECKLIST

- It should have a leaf-patterned or dull finish to avoid detection from the wary eyes of wild turkeys.
- It might hold a sling to free your hands for using friction calls while standing, as you attempt to make cold-call contact with turkeys, or to simply help you walk out of the woods unencumbered.
- It should deliver a tight, swarming pellet pattern at optimum shotgun range (20–35 yards in my book—choke, load, and gauge depending). As mentioned, test your shotgun with various turkey loads and screw-in choke tubes to determine how it will handle when afield.
- It might have a short barrel for maneuverability, weigh as light as possible to hold steady while a wild turkey burns a stare through you, and be just heavy enough to ease the recoil shock of a magnum load on your shoulder.
- It should fit in your arms and rest against your shoulder as if part of your physical frame, and feel so right there that you can deliver one killing shot with informed confidence based on experience and preparation.

Turkey load selection, shotgun patterning, and proper shot placement create autumn scenes like this one at Turkey Trot Acres in upstate New York.

Choke up. Experiment with options if your shotgun permits. A particular choke might work well with one load but not another. Extra-Full and Full chokes are the typical options for turkey hunters since a dense concentration of pellets is desired.

Seated, and from a stationary position, shoot first to determine point of aim (any size load will do initially). Do so at a paper target roughly 10 yards away. Ask yourself, is the pattern centered, or off? If the shot charge is off, is it way high, low, left, or right? To fix this, some hunters employ scopes or sights to adjust for such discrepancies. Then again, your shooting form might also be blamed.

After you've determined point of aim, move the turkey-head patterning target to 20 yards, and fire your loads. Some prefer to do so from the stationary position they used to determine point of aim. Others sit as they would in the turkey woods. Study how each different load option varies. If possible, shoot different shells through various firearms to see the results.

Shoot loads at different yardage distances: 10, 20, 30, and 40. Density will obviously change. Your maximum distance is determined when fewer if any pellets fail to hit the head and neck area of that paper target. If that happens at 40 yards, consider only shooting turkeys at a closer maximum distance.

Experiment with chokes if your shotgun permits it. A particular choke might work well with one load but not another. Extra-Full and Full chokes are the typical options for turkey hunters since a dense concentration of pellets is desired.

Penetration is also important to note. Shoot old phone books, or through old plywood with your range of shells. Shoot, shoot, and shoot some more. Know what your gun will do. In the end, one shot is required, but it takes a lot to make it.

THE RIFLE QUESTION

I haven't shot a fall turkey with a rifle—legal in my native Keystone State—since the 1970s. It's not the most efficient way of anchoring a bird, though some astute riflemen find ways to ensure that (head shots, for instance). In most fall and winter turkey states it's not legal. Some places it is, largely due to lingering tradition.

Marksmen can indeed fix their aim point on the turkey's head, the way we do with tightly choked shotguns. This way you either hit and down the turkey directly with a punch to its walnut-sized brainpan, or you miss. It's a small but sure target. Those who choose to shoot the wing butt often find that turkey will run, fly, and sail away, only most likely to die later, and out of reach—especially if it hits the bird just slightly off the mark. A spine shot will anchor the bird, but a near miss surely won't. There's little room for error either way.

Hunting with a rifle can put you at an advantage for when you draw birds in, but just out of would-be shotgun range—something all of us see routinely when pursuing turkeys. A 50-yard head shot on a standing bird is manageable with a rifle and swiftly downs the turkey, so long as the aim is true and the bullet isn't deflected on the way. You need to know about turkey behavior in order to pick the best shot as it presents itself. Motionless, standing birds qualify. Moving, head-jerking turkeys don't.

Target practice will increase confidence. Accuracy will rule in the field. Scopes might also offer an additional boost to your effort. As range goes, stay within your shooting limits, ability depending. Anything longer is a stunt, and could result in a crippling loss. Again, the pleasure is in pulling turkeys close.

The history of turkey literature surely reflects rifle hunting, as both Edward McIlhenny, Charles Jordan, and Henry Davis include mention in their works. Only you honestly know whether its limitations are extended by your marksmanship abilities.

The same holds true for those who favor muzzleloaders. Frontstuffers are an acquired taste, and for some, they improve the feel of the game in some satisfying ways, making the hunt more of a challenge.

ARCHERY TACKLE

As a kid, I attempted to draw my dad's longbow and recurve back, full of fascination and awe. I knew that these hunting tools had allowed him to take deer at close range. He did it from an apple tree back then: no elaborate stand, just a plank of wood between two thick limbs. His broadheads, sharp as shaving razors, exuded a seriousness somewhat different than rifle cartridges or shotgun shells, their lethal potential exposed on blades. For anyone who hunts with a bow, this connection is somewhat primal and definitely primitive in today's modern world.

Some of us like this throwback connection. Maybe it's the quiet simplicity of bowhunting. I've navigated both the modern and traditional bow options over the years. As one who hunts the generous 101-day New Hampshire fall turkey season that begins in mid-September (archery tackle only), and ends ten days before Christmas, such gear is the ticket into the autumn turkey woods.

Now let's get one thing straight: using a bow and arrow is not the best way to drop a wild turkey during special archery-only turkey hunts around the country. Calling the bird into range is only part of the deal, whereas doing that with a shotgun would about close it.

For instance, some 342 wild turkeys were arrowed by New Hampshire archers during the fall of 2004. The three-month, archery-only season yielded 205 hens and 137 gobblers (Sept. 15–Dec. 15). One year later, the fall 2005 harvest accounted for 296 bow-tackle birds during the same time period. This consistency reflects both inherent difficulty and possibility in a northern New England state that holds 30,000 turkeys. You can take a fall bird with an arrow, but it's not easy.

Missing birds with a sharp-tipped stick in what would be easy gun range is routine—at least for me. And yes, I satisfy the innate desire to tag an autumn turkey in states like Vermont and New York where not only is a firearm legal, but also a dog. Even New Hampshire—a longtime archery-only location—added a five-day shotgun season in the fall of 2006. Legal strategies vary widely everywhere you go, and you adapt accordingly. In several states, I'm a fall turkey hunter who uses a bow because that's the only legal way to do it during special seasons. In others I use a shotgun and a dog, too.

Times change. I tote carbon arrows now, not the old standard aluminum models I started out with. Since shooting a compound bow is akin to what we do when rifle hunting, it's all teched-up with the usual details: peep sight, sight pins, prong-style arrow rest, the works. Traditional archers know that using a recurve or longbow is analogous to shooting a shotgun. It's instinctive. Stick bows don't afford the let-off option that compounds do. And you need that little cheat to draw (and hold) on a wild turkey, especially us creaky-jointed forty-somethings. Sure enough, you can shoot a bow from inside a concealing blind (especially on patterned birds), but hunting game out there in the open is appealing, too.

A DOZEN BOWHUNTING TURKEY BASICS

1. Get the turkey close—real close. Ten to twenty yards is a reliable shooting range.
2. Use a manmade blind constructed from natural materials on patterned turkeys to conceal your movements (though it limits mobility), or hunt with a model that's easy to transport and assemble.
3. Arrow a 3-D turkey target on a regular basis to visualize your intended quarry.
4. Stake turkey decoys at your effective bow range to fix a flock's or individual bird's position.
5. Choose turkey-specific mechanical broadheads for solid flight and serious cutting diameter.
6. Time your shot on a calm, standing turkey in range with a sure draw and arrow release.
7. Practice shooting from a hunting stool, a standing position, or on your backside to reflect hunting conditions.
8. Place your shots at the neck's base on facing birds, and at the anal vent when turkeys face away.
9. Wear reliable, comfortable camouflage to instill confidence and concealment in your game plan.
10. After anchoring a turkey, place your bow down, then quickly approach and step on the flopping bird's head or neck before removing the arrow if it hasn't passed through.
11. Hunt archery-only seasons to extend your opportunities, and for the intangible pleasures such outings offer.
12. Don't stress too much over missed shots, as it's part of the archery turkey experience.

It's almost always fun. The goal of every hunter is to secure the bird or animal he's after, of course. Still, I enjoy the inadvertent catch-and-release aspect of the deal (I can hear you routinely successful turkey archers snickering). Good memories sustain.

On missing, I typically chuckle to myself, and then start muttering. The turkeys, they just keep on going, oblivious to any of my emotion-laced grumbling. An unidentified presence has thrown a stick at them, and they aren't asking any questions.

WHEN TO SHOOT

Once you know what to shoot, you have to decide when to do it in a live situation. My dog had flushed a late afternoon Empire State flock in a sloping pasture corner right before it rained all night, and hard. The next morning a buddy and I drove the shower-slick roads looking for field flocks. Then it occurred to us that revisiting the original site wouldn't be such a bad idea, especially since the weather forecast called for clearing skies.

Then the sun broke. Hallelujah. Since my Midge had done her job the day before and was just this side of tired, we decided to slink down in there ourselves to see if the flock had yet to gather where we last saw them, letting her rest back in the truck. "There, a turkey," my hunting buddy hissed from our trail-sneaking position, as I glimpsed the wad of standing birds. Ever hear two men running and barking like dogs? Our flush attempt wasn't half bad.

Not two minutes later, almost too soon to sit down and get ready, we heard kee-keeing over the near rise. We mimicked the birds: my buddy wide right, seated with his back to a broad tree trunk, and me facing left about five yards away. Two dark forms—a pair of juvenile turkeys—fishhooked in, then appeared down my shotgun barrel. I watched as they minced steps in shoulder to shoulder. Taking two New York fall turkeys in one day was perfectly legal, so without a thought, I waited for their heads and necks to coincide, then pulled the trigger before they got too close. Two October turkeys down; tags filled.

"I thought maybe you would wait to see if we could double," he deadpanned. Ouch. Deciding when to pull the trigger can affect friendships in unexpected ways. Selfish of me? Yeah, a little.

"Listen," I said, "there's an adult hen yelping down in the woods," a bird my buddy eventually called into range, and dropped.

"Mine's bigger," he said, smiling, and with that, we high-fived.

A wild turkey steps into shotgun or bow range. Scouting, locating, calling, and reducing the weight of your wallet have all paid off. But suddenly, that black eye drills you. The big bird flicks its wings and turns. It's now or never. A second or two later might just mean never. Planning when to pull the trigger or release the arrow is crucial. It's important to know when to say when.

If you're not under pressure from a calling turkey that's approaching your setup, step off distances to landmarks before getting in position. This is especially important while turkey dogging, as it's hard to move both you and your canine. Note the distances to clearings, hilltops, brushy cover, and trees, and then study landmarks at the limit of your range. If you're hunting with a buddy, determine which direction you'll shoot in.

To know when to pull the trigger, pattern your load, choke, and shotgun using life-size head and neck turkey targets. Shoot from various distances. Count target hits. Gain confidence in your firepower. It's one less thing to think about when that turkey steps into range.

If possible, set up against a tree that is as least as wide as your shoulders and as high as your head. Make sure you have a clear view of your shooting range in front of you, and to each side. If you're hunting with a buddy, know where he's sitting. Establish ranges in which you'll shoot.

After you've stepped off distances, settle into position. If a turkey is calling, and moving toward your setup, point your shotgun or bow in the direction that you last heard the bird. When that turkey appears, use the landmarks as a reference for the distance of the shot. Limit your movement, and adjust your position only when the turkey's head is obscured behind cover. Take the shot only when the bird is in range, when your quarry's head and neck are completely exposed, and the target has been fully identified.

Hand-held range finders can give precise yardage readings if you'd rather not take the time to measure distance with steps, or you don't trust your judgment. Riflemen and big game archers routinely use range–

Before a wild turkey ever approaches your setup, make an imagined picture of when you'll shoot. Consider a variety of live hunting scenarios—the bird marching in from the left, sneaking in from the right, coming straight in, or from directly behind you. Turkeys will often make moves you hadn't planned on. Listen. Watch. Anticipate.

finders, and turkey hunters can, too. Practice testing this tool before the hunt though. You and a buddy can wager friendly bets on shooting distances—say during a gun-patterning or arrow-flinging session—and learn as you go.

KNOW YOUR GUN, BOW, LOAD, AND ARROW

As implied earlier, shoot your shotgun with various loads at comfortable distances—an exercise that should be an under-40-yard game; 25 to 35 steps is even better (and with archery tackle, try to pull them even closer). A turkey can only be cleanly dropped with a shotgun when drilled in the skull and neck. Body shots generally only cripple wild turkeys since their vitals are protected by feather and muscle, though capable archers chance at better success. Wounding a wild turkey is to be avoided, though unfortunately it can happen. Minimize that chance. Occasional ego-driven turkey-camp monologues about 60-yard shots are pure bunk. Ignore such talk.

To know when to pull the trigger, pattern your load, choke, and shotgun using life-size head and neck turkey targets. Shoot from various distances. Count target hits. Gain confidence in your firepower. It's one less thing to think about when that turkey steps into range. If you bowhunt, shoot regularly to get a feel for your equipment so that you might seal the deal in the moment of truth. Develop that muscle memory.

Okay. You've patterned your gun, choke, and preferred turkey load to determine effective range before your hunt. During the hunt, don't fire at a bird beyond that distance. Many of my hunting buddies like to say that 40 is the magic number for yardage (most tote 12-gauges). Some turkeys will only come so far though. If a turkey is at marginal range, let the bird drift away, or try to call it closer. Patience is the key. Be disciplined.

If you're pinned down, let the regrouping flock move past you. Wait for the bird you want to pass behind a tree, then raise your gun or draw your bow. If the turkey keeps moving, cluck to get its head up. Shoot when the bird pauses. Don't rush. Don't panic. Enjoy those final moments. Turkeys at close range are a sight to see—enjoy it.

Before a wild turkey ever approaches your setup, make an imagined picture of when you'll shoot. Make the mental shot in your mind before you pull the shotgun's trigger or release that arrow. Consider a variety of live hunting scenarios—the bird marching in from the left, sneaking in from the right, coming straight in, or from directly behind you. Turkeys will often make moves you hadn't planned on. Listen. Watch. Anticipate. Be ready to adapt, and know where you can make your shots. Think it through.

Shooter's tip: While waiting to make your move, sit comfortably with your shotgun's forend resting on your raised knee, facing in the direction you think the turkey will come from. If your firearm is equipped with a sling, place that carrying aid's shoulder padding between the gun and your knee for added comfort.

KNOW YOUR TARGET

Don't shoot at mere wild turkey sounds, colors, or movements. Identify physical characteristics of the bird: head, beard (or no beard), breast feathers (black-tipped for a gobbler; brown-tipped for a hen), and feet (pink for an adult turkey; brown for a juvenile). Use these details to compose a full visual picture. Wait until you see the entire turkey, not just parts of the bird. Again, only shoot the head and neck when that fall hen or gobbler is in range.

While waiting for turkeys to appear, settle into your setup, and try not to move for extended periods of time: your shotgun's forend resting on your left knee (if you're a right-handed gunner), eyeing the woods for a bird coming into view. Camouflage will give you the confidence that

When suspicious, wild turkeys will drill you with their one-eyed stare. They'll flick their wing tips. They'll putt, pirouette, and stride away. Once you've been detected, the game is in its final seconds. If your bird is out of range, let it go. If you have a clean shot, take it—now. JOHN HAFNER PHOTO

turkeys can't see you, and sitting still without moving will focus your thinking.

Shooter's tip: Wear your watch face on the inside of the wrist holding your shotgun's forend. That way you can note the time—especially legal shooting hours—without moving too much. A glance will do it, especially if turkeys are working to your calls. Some fall turkey states such as New York open hunting at legal sunrise, often 10 to 15 minutes after turkeys fly off the roost, and close shooting at legal sunset, which sometimes occurs when birds are still on the ground.

As the turkey approaches, move the muzzle of your gun with imperceptible ease, but stay trained on the turkey's head and neck. Drift ever so slowly with the bird's movements, as it passes behind trees that block the view of you, the human hunter. When it steps into range, take a second to concentrate, imagine the shot, and then pull the trigger (or release the arrow). Anticipate when you'll make the shot based on your guess as to what the turkey will do.

When suspicious, wild turkeys will drill you with their one-eyed stare. They'll flick their wing tips. They'll putt, pirouette, and stride away.

Some clubs, camps, and lodges conduct pre-hunt discussions. Allow time to exchange ideas in this setting, say at the supper table, or some other comfortable situation.

Once you've been detected, the game is in its final seconds. If your bird is out of range, let it go. If you have a clean shot, take it—now. Focus, and shoot the back of the head, or laugh it off that you've been beaten. Regroup, and then make another game plan.

TRUST YOUR GUIDE

If you hunt with and hire out professional turkey guides, trust their judgment when they call the shot—within reason, of course. These hard-working folks deal with a variety of hunters, from the absolutely inexperienced to the veteran gunner, but often the former rather than the latter. In the end, though, you pull the trigger.

If possible, meet with the guide before going afield, and discuss your preferences for the hunt. Listen to him, too. Ideally your hunting guide should know your gun's limitations, the ammo you're using, and your experience level.

If you feel uncomfortable taking shots beyond 40 yards, tell the guide. If you like to call birds ten steps closer, let him know. Doing so after he whispers, "kill it" with the wary turkey in plain sight isn't the best time. If you only want to take a bird you call in, ask if that person can direct you to the location, and with him along, let you work those turkeys. It's your hunt, after all. Some outfits conduct pre-hunt lodge discussions the night before clients and guides go out. If the turkey camp you're visiting doesn't allow time to exchange ideas in this setting, suggest it at the supper table, or some other comfortable situation.

Remember, this is supposed to be fun. Pressing too hard has a way of translating into a lack of hunting success—both shooting, and otherwise. Turkey fever—the sudden, undeniable racing of your heart and failure to stay calm when you need to react—along with the opposite exaggerated nonchalance of not being fully prepared, will make you miss shots and fail to close the deal. Bear down at the moment of truth and squeeze off the shot. You've worked too hard to arrive at that opportunity to blow it.

A turkey in range is a memorable thing. Make the most of it by taking a well-placed, clean shot within the limits of your gun, your ammo, your bow, and its arrow.

CHAPTER 16

Put some thought into choosing shooting lanes that offer a broad view from your setup.

Safety Sense

It's the first weekend of fall turkey season and a well-deserved day outdoors. As luck would have it, you've broken a small flock of super jakes on foot in a semi-rural wildlife management area in farm country and established a setup near the base of a broad-trunked oak. There you wait the better part of an hour, satisfied with your effort. You offer some raspy three-noted yelps. No birds answer, which isn't all that uncommon when dealing with fall gobblers. Still, you call again and soon hear leaves crunching over a nearby hilly rise. There, you think to yourself, one's coming in silently, without calling. You get your shotgun up and sight down the barrel, certain that it's a turkey moving to the flush site.

You squint to the right and see red, bobbing red on the hillside through leafy cover. You fixate your attention on the shooting lane where you expect the bird to step out into view thirty yards in front of you. Your pulse bounces. You calm down a bit, breathe deep, settle in, and cluck once, clicking the safety off. The red daub, now paired with a moving blob of black, moves through the wooded October cover. You envision taking the shot. The turkey is coming in on a leash.

Just a few more steps and . . . what soon materializes makes your face flush hot and your arms tingle with an electrical shock. It's a young girl wearing a black jacket and red knit cap, slowly maneuvering her bicycle along the groomed trail. A wave of nausea hits you as she pedals away.

You snap the safety back on, ashamed at the near mistake, which is too mild a word in such an instance. Think it can't happen to you? Think again.

Wait to see the entire wild turkey until you shoot. The biggest problem, of course, is your confidence that the specific color, expected movement, correct shape, and credible sound of an approaching object matches that of your quarry. It's hard to tell your engaged mind otherwise. JOHN HAFNER PHOTO

Wait to see the entire wild turkey until you shoot. Period. The biggest problem, of course, is your confidence that the specific color, expected movement, correct shape, and credible sound of an approaching object matches that of your quarry. It's hard to tell your engaged mind otherwise.

When you hear a sound, always think that it might be another hunter or someone in the woods until visual evidence indicates otherwise. Early fall leaves in wooded areas can sometimes inhibit this ability.

While hunter education classes instill a certain safety sense, applying that knowledge and information while afield is yet another thing entirely. Don't let ego make you shoot when you shouldn't (this also goes for unwarranted trigger pulls on wild turkeys out of range). You don't have to kill a bird that day. It's okay to be carrying a tag at the end of the season. Life goes on. A shooting error stays with you forever.

When you hear a sound, always think that it might be another hunter approaching your position, or someone in the woods, until visual evidence indicates otherwise.

EITHER-SEX HUNTS

Most autumn and winter turkey seasons offer opportunities to take birds of either sex. While target identification during the spring gobbler season is certainly important, it's a dual challenge during the woodstove months.

In spring, many hunters offer hen yelps to arouse the attention of nearby gobblers that are seeking out the company of female turkeys for breeding. In fall and winter, sportsmen offer those same turkey sounds, with plenty of variations. Since every turkey call you make is that of a legal bird, visual identification rules. It bears repeating that shooting at mere turkey sounds is definitely out. The dark lump of a turkey hunter calling from the base of a tree might look like a stationary bird. Tell your mind otherwise until visual evidence is certain. Positively identify your target before slipping off the safety. In the lead scenario, that hypothetical hunter did not.

It's not only important to aim at the turkey's head and make a sure killing shot, but it's also required that you note what's beyond that bird in the event of a miss—even with a trigger pull that connects (they call it a scattergun for a reason).

Put some thought into choosing shooting lanes that offer a broad view from your setup. Where will pellets go? Would they chance at hitting another member of your hunting party? Might the shot charge ricochet? Arrows are definitely known for doing this when flung at a passing turkey, only to skip off deadfall on the ground and carry beyond the intended target.

And never ever point your gun at something you don't intend to shoot, even if that firearm is unloaded. It's also wise to choose hunting buddies who take such safety issues seriously.

DECOY SETS

Fake turkeys are intended to draw other birds in and hold them long enough for you to take a shot. Sometimes, however, they draw hunter attention, too. For safety's sake, either choose not to use decoys at all in the fall and winter, since it's often legal to take turkeys of either sex, or if you do, stake your fakes in such a way that an errant shot might not endanger you. Setups should include a broad-trunked tree at your back—one of the things the hunter in the lead section did correctly. If the area you hunt is busy (public areas are like this, surely), opt not to use decoys, or simply hunt somewhere else.

Devices to instill movement in plastic and foam hens and gobblers are available, but you might think otherwise if the season you're hunting permits longer-range firearms such as rifles.

CALLING IN HUNTERS

It happens. You see a guy stalking your calling, crouched low and easing steadily toward your position. Don't move, but shout, "Hey, hunter here." When he looks, say it again. If he keeps coming, say it a third time until he stops and moves away. Or not. Occasionally the person will wander up and begin an apologetic conversation. You meet all kinds.

When targeting a new or even a familiar location, first note vehicles at the designated parking spots and those trucks pulled off in unusual areas. And just because you don't see a car doesn't mean a turkey hunter isn't in there with you.

I've been the guest of friends who have taken me onto private land that was supposed to be open only to us, only to find hunters there. My hosts were correct in saying that they had permission, but the trespassers either disregarded such things as posted signs and locked gates, or the well-meaning but busy landowner failed to communicate that others were also given permission.

At any rate, if you find yourself in a situation where hunters are stalking your position, shout. Yell. Bark out a command. Forget that your hunt is momentarily finished. Never move or wave your arms, as the shape and color—some forms of camouflage are obviously way too dark for safety-minded taste—might promote a mistaken-for-game event.

BEER AND BUGS

Having a cold beer has a time and a place for some, surely—not in the field, though. Not while hunting. This goes for controlled substances as well. Writing these words feels slightly foolish given the obviousness of the warning, but I can easily recall a turkey camp conversation about so-and-so and his tendency to pass time in the woods by popping a few tops. Stupid.

The dangers of insect-borne diseases are well documented, and the Internet has plenty of reliable, peer-reviewed sources to search out, so I won't include them here. Put simply, some of us apply bug spray to our face mask and hat, the back sides of both hands, then rub the residue on

It happens fast. You see a blur of movement, hunters stalking your calling, moving steadily toward your position. Don't move, but shout, "Hey, hunter here."

our neck and temples—the places that mosquitoes find on warm autumn days when you're sitting still as a turkey approaches.

In my experience, hunter clothing that includes some sort of implied bug proofing such a tick cuffs often only promotes the blasted things to climb your body to your neck and head. Head nets do avert mosquitoes to an extent, and turkey buds claim that such tools as ThermaCELL units do actually keep bugs away (these portable, odor-free aids operate on a butane cartridge and with repellant mats). As ticks go, check yourself— and your turkey dog, if you hunt with one—after every outing if you live in bug-challenged areas. Many of us do.

OTHER SAFETY TIPS

Repositioning: Sometimes you have to move close to a field to determine whether flocks you've patterned are using it. Sometimes you've called a bird and it's drifted away, possibly joining others. Scenarios like this often happen to turkey hunters, so be careful whenever you move from one position to another. Try to take a broad view of your situation. Is it likely other hunters are using an area? Is the turkey you hear answering you actually a turkey? Some folks use walkie-talkies where legal to communicate turkey movement and their own. Some states even require the use of hunter orange clothing while moving and when established at your setup.

Camouflage: Cover your entire body with the stuff. I'm routinely alarmed at seeing turkey hunters (possibly new to the game, or stubborn in their ways) walking about in blue jeans (the color of a hen's head, or an excited gobbler's face), or a hat with red in it, or a plaid shirt containing red, white, and blue. And if you only think that spring gobbler heads bear this color, you're wrong. I've seen fall toms bent on fighting for pecking order status that had their brick-red heads flare red, white, and blue just prior to a fight with another bird.

Dressing down might be deemed "hunter casual" in some circles, or just downright lazy, but you should look and act the part. Avoid the possibility—remote but plausible—of having a hunter view part of your clothing as the shape and color of a turkey. If you're like me, you look better in camouflage anyway.

Bird in hand: You've done well. You've gotten a fall or winter turkey in hand, and met with success. If you didn't right after the shot, click that gun's safety back on. Great job. Now you have to get it out of the woods—safely.

Carrying the tagged bird over your shoulder works well in choreographed photos, the so-called hero shots of our tradition (some of which are contained in this book), and surely the wildlife art of our time, but during the actual post-hunt period that turkey should be placed in your field vest. To do so, take the head and neck and fold it under a wing. Ease the tagged bird into the game bag at the back of your vest. The solid weight there feels good as you walk out to your truck, and you'll be safer for it.

Crossing fences: If you are crossing a fence or some other obstruction, control your firearm. If you're alone, unload the gun; place it over or through the fence by leaning it against a tree on the other side or laying it on the ground. Proceed to cross there yourself. If hunting with a buddy, hold his firearm as he moves to the other side, then pass yours and his back to him before you do the same.

Unload the gun: If you intend to flush nearby birds on foot in an effort to call separated flock members back to the site, put your gun down in a place where you can find it again, or unload it before running up on the turkeys.

If you are turkey dogging, only load the gun after the flock has been flushed and you're installed in your blind—unless you plan on trying to take one on the break. If so, keep an eye on that canine.

Dog safety: If you're hunting your dog in a high-traffic area, seek out birds away from the road. If others unfamiliar with the turkey dogging tradition are hunting the area, put an orange vest on that canine. All my English setters have plume-like tails, and my Midge is almost pure white. White. Tail. Need I say more?

Cell phones: It's a good idea to carry a cell phone in case of emergencies, but turn it off during your hunt if you don't want calls at unexpected times. Tell a family member where you'll be and when you expect to arrive home. Use walkie-talkies to communicate with hunting buddies during big woods hunts.

Life's short. Hunt hard. Be safe while you do it.

CHAPTER 17

The author is the only one wearing a beard in this photo. Most fall and winter states permit turkey hunters to tag either-sex birds.

Fall and Winter
Where-To

"In the spring we hunt gobblers, and in the fall we hunt turkeys," a friend of mine likes to say. Historically, the roots of wild turkey hunting are in autumn and winter. These modern days, however, state-based wildlife managers often emphasize spring gobbler hunting, while also determining appropriate fall and/or winter seasons for this special gamebird.

In truth, management decisions are economically motivated, based on biological data, and influenced by public opinion. Still, only a handful of states choose not to offer opportunities outside of spring gobbler season. Fortunately, the story of American wild turkey restoration is a positive one, with turkeys now widely available for hunters to enjoy on a nearly year-round basis. Maine's spring gobbler opportunities, for instance, end the first week of June—the latest running season in the country. Nationwide, only the months of July and August—the time when brood hens raise poults—hold no wild turkey hunting.

Sometimes these seasons are influenced by turkey population estimates (a challenge in itself). Often geographical location and hunter numbers are modifying factors. In areas of the Northeast and Mid-Atlantic states where the autumn turkey hunt is a notable pastime, season length is a management tool. Elsewhere, in the Midwest for instance, license quotas help biologists limit hunter numbers to control turkey populations and the influences on them. Bag limits, plus the length and timing of turkey seasons, are also considered as well as the legal method of taking a bird.

At turkey camp, kick back, relax, and double-check game laws. Management approaches and turkey-hunting regulations vary from state to state. It's important to track informational changes.

Hardcore fall turkey hunters, and much of the sport's tradition, exist in places like upstate New York, Pennsylvania, and the Virginias.

AUTUMN STATES

October, with its painted hardwoods and visible field flocks, is the time we fall turkey hunters live for. While some seasons commence a month before, our calendar's tenth month is the time many autumn offerings are available to hunters.

Hardcore fall turkey hunters, and much of the sport's tradition, exist in places like upstate New York, my native Pennsylvania, and the Virginias. As flock populations have grown over the past decades, opportunities have expanded in locations like Ohio, Michigan, Kentucky, Tennessee, and elsewhere. Missouri's season runs throughout October. The presence of the Eastern wild turkey over half the United States has promoted and sustained an autumn tradition where it is found, as this subspecies is the most widespread.

Fringe areas, where the post-restoration tradition is newer, often offer archery-only seasons on wild turkeys, which coincide with bowhunting

Missouri's fall turkey season runs throughout October. Terry Head shoulders a Show-Me-State longbeard.

Places like Montana, Wyoming, and the Dakotas offer turkey seasons into early winter, when snowfall is a regular feature. Here the author peers from behind a snowy day Merriam's longbeard.

whitetails. In northern New England, Maine and New Hampshire are good examples of this management approach.

Fall seasons are scheduled where Merriam's and Rio Grande turkeys roam, often coinciding with the hunting of big game species—of course, some states deem the wild turkey "small game," but gobbler and hen hunters know otherwise.

In places like Texas, various autumn and winter seasons for flocks run into the New Year, location and "method of take" depending. Florida and its Osceola subspecies (though the panhandle has Easterns) is "bearded birds only," a management approach that promotes autumn and winter turkey hunting, with a specific limitation. Archery, muzzle-loader, crossbow, and general firearms seasons fall into place throughout this September though January period.

Since the establishment and development of fall hunting opportunities is ongoing and somewhat unpredictable, routinely study what your particular state is planning for the upcoming season. At times, as an interested sportsman, you can influence this process with your insight and enthusiasm. Chances are some autumn turkey hunt—often commencing or ongoing in October—is available in your state, or within road-tripping distance.

WINTER STATES

Places like Montana, Wyoming, and the Dakotas offer turkey seasons into early winter, when snowfall is a regular feature. Kansas, Virginia, and North Carolina provide a chance for winter turkey hunters to slake their enthusiasm during January hunts. As management intent goes, such opportunities are often staged around firearms seasons for deer, placed before or after that particular annual phase.

The aim? To both satisfy the sportsman, but also to control and limit the take of wild turkeys on an incidental basis. Some states do provide archery-only hunts when deer and turkey seasons coincide, and in these locations, the method of take is a dominant management feature.

FALL AND WINTER TURKEY SEASONS:
OPENING/CLOSING MONTHS (2006–2007)
United States

Check your current state regulations for recent changes.

Alabama: November–January
Alaska: No fall or winter season
Arizona: September–October
Arkansas: October–February
California: November
Colorado: September–October

Connecticut: September–December
Delaware: No fall or winter season
Florida: September–January
Georgia: No fall or winter season
Hawaii: November–January
Idaho: September–October
Illinois: October–January
Indiana: October
Iowa: October–January
Kansas: October–January
Kentucky: September-December
Louisiana: No fall or winter season
Maine: October
Maryland: October–November
Massachusetts: October–November
Michigan: October–November
Minnesota: October
Mississippi: October–December
Missouri: October
Montana: September–January
Nebraska: October–November
Nevada: October
New Hampshire: September–December
New Jersey: October–November
New Mexico: September
New York: October–November
North Carolina: January
North Dakota: October–January
Ohio: October–November
Oklahoma: October–January
Oregon: October–December
Pennsylvania: October–November
Rhode Island: October
South Carolina: No fall or winter season
South Dakota: October–December
Tennessee: November–December
Texas: October–February
Utah: No fall or winter season
Vermont: October–November
Virginia: October–January
Washington: September–December

All-terrain vehicles will get you where you need to go in big country.

West Virginia: October–November
Wisconsin: October–November
Wyoming: September–December

Canada

Canada is on the northern fringe of the wild turkey's range. As of this writing, two fall seasons are offered in provinces bordering the United States.

British Columbia: September
Manitoba: October

TURKEY DOGGING STATES

As stated in this book, a well-trained dog is a tool to help a hunter find and flush a turkey flock more efficiently. That canine is only effective if handled by a competent turkey hunter. Using dogs to pursue other forms of winged upland game is a longstanding tradition, of course. Opportunities to hunt wild turkeys in the company of a canine are increasing as of this writing. In the early 1990s, only eleven states allowed turkey dogging. A decade later, that number had doubled.

Some fall turkey hunters document their trip by video.

Some states permit the use of dogs as a byproduct of other forms of upland bird hunting. In other words, since wild turkey seasons often coincide with those opportunities for ruffed grouse, ring-necked pheasants, and the like, management officials also deem dogging flocks legal. Places like Vermont and Michigan's Upper Peninsula are good examples, as autumn turkey seasons run concurrent to annual grouse and woodcock dates.

Other states such as Virginia, West Virginia, and New York, permit the use of turkey dogs due to an established and ongoing tradition, which isn't so much a byproduct of other upland hunting but the preferred approach.

In recent years, states such as New Jersey, Ohio, Kentucky, Kansas, and others have legalized the strategy. As I write this, Nevada specifically prohibits the use of dogs during spring turkey hunts, but resists declaring

On the open road . . . winter turkey seasons are available around the country.

it legal or illegal in fall, while Rhode Island has proposed permitting the use of dogs for the estimated 6,000 autumn turkeys there, though it's not official as yet. This trend owes much to expanded flock populations and educational awareness of the turkey dogging tradition.

The tradition of finding and flushing flocks is officially legal in the following 23 states and single Canadian province:

California
Colorado
Hawaii
Idaho
Iowa
Kansas
Kentucky
Maryland
Michigan
Montana
Nebraska
New Jersey

New York
North Carolina
North Dakota
Ohio
Oregon
Tennessee
Texas
Vermont
Virginia
West Virginia
Wyoming
British Columbia

As a turkey hunter, it not only pays to scout areas you plan on hunting, but also to study state-based websites to monitor opportunities. One efficient way to do this in the off-season—say between the end of spring outings and the start of fall hunts—is to bookmark specific online sites on your computer. This way, you can routinely note legislation aimed at

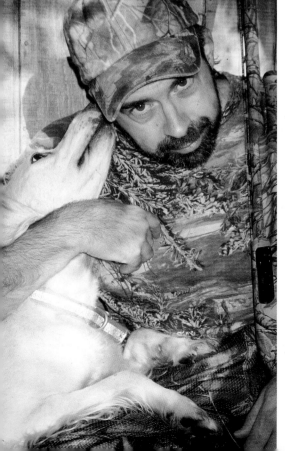

In the early 1990s, only eleven states allowed turkey dogging. Twenty-three states and one Canadian province now permit it, while proposals to legalize in other locations are ongoing. English setter Midge, the author's hunting buddy, offers some advice.

Kansas, Virginia, and North Carolina provide a chance for winter turkey hunters to slake their enthusiasm during January hunts, where the use of dogs is also legal.

increasing (or decreasing) turkey seasons, as some fluctuate. You can also plan hunts around specific dates, check permit deadlines, and note additional requirements as you bridge the end of one season and the start of the next one.

FROM FIELD TO TABLE

You've worked hard to tag a wild turkey. If you want to enjoy that bird back at camp or home, steps need to be taken. Here are some suggestions:

Clean your turkey ASAP. To field dress a bird, put the turkey on its back. Insert your knife at the bottom of the breastbone, and cut an opening. Reach in and remove all entrails. Some hunters chill the open cavity with a bag of ice during transport or short-term storage, assuming the turkey isn't dressed and processed directly.

Do you want to pluck or skin your bird? Hunters pluck turkeys to later deep-fry the bird whole, smoke it, or roast it in a conventional oven. Dipping the turkey in a pot of boiling water will allow you to remove the feathers easily. Do this outside, of course. First dip, holding the feet, and then carefully lift it out. Pull the feathers off directly (gloves help, and it will be hot to the touch). It goes much faster if one person holds the bird

To fillet the breasts, put the bird on its back. Remove enough breast feathers to lift the skin up, and make a small cut to pull the skin down on both sides, exposing the meat. Now breast the turkey, making cuts along the breastbone on both sides to lift out the meat in two whole pieces, one per side.

To satisfy your desire to turkey hunt widely and often, you travel. Airlines can put you into some of the best places.

and others pluck. If you like fried, smoked, or roasted turkey skin, this is a great option.

To fillet the breasts, put the bird on its back. Remove enough breast feathers to lift the skin up and make a small cut to pull the skin down on both sides, exposing the meat. Now breast the turkey, making cuts along the breastbone on both sides to lift out the meat in two whole pieces, one per side. To remove leg and thigh meat, repeat the skinning process, then cut through the thigh muscle near the bird's back. Grab the leg and lift it until the joint pops. Carefully use the knife if needed.

After these steps, meat can be frozen in camp for transport home. If you've opted to skin your bird, breast meat can later be cut into chunks, fingers, or cooked in larger pieces. Drumsticks make superb soups if you first parboil them in a pot of boiling water, and then remove the meat after cooling.

As always, it's important to check specific state regulations before cleaning, dressing, and transporting your turkey.

TURKEY TRAVEL
To satisfy your desire to hunt widely and often, you travel. To do so, you need to take plenty of necessary gear with you. Sure, there's that exaggerated gender-specific notion that vacationing women need a space the size

It sounds basic, but always remember to get precise directions to turkey camp. Without this important information, your late arrival is almost assured.

of an empty railroad car to lug their excessive travel belongings in, while most men can get by with a shoebox. Well, not if that guy is traveling to turkey hunt.

First of all, there's the firearm to deal with. As this goes, nothing much has changed since 9/11. Traveling hunters have always had to declare guns and bows, and as a rule, it mostly works without a hitch. Sometimes you pass through in heavy, awkward silence. Sometimes the distance between those who hunt and those who don't hunt is vocally palpable.

Take the fellow air traveler in the baggage-check line that once asked me if I had a musical instrument inside my lengthy hard case. When I replied, "No, an unloaded shotgun for turkey hunting," he took a dramatic step back, his face blushing.

Sometimes you have to play teacher and explain the rules to airport officials. They have to check to see that the shotgun is unloaded, and you have to declare that it's safe with your signature and date on a blaze-orange card, which goes inside the gun case. Sometimes they let you lock it with supervision. Sometimes they take the key, inspect the firearm, and

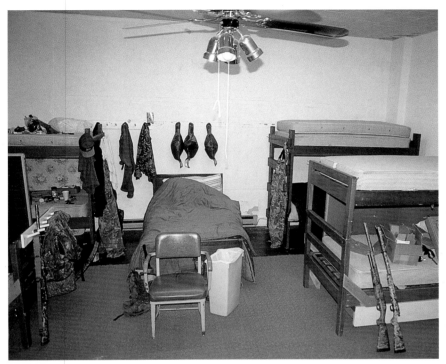

The best turkey camps offer all you really need: a place to sleep and store your gear.

then lock it up for you. This all takes some time, which is fine, but it draws attention to you. Stay cool. Be courteous and polite. If you travel enough, all this is expected.

That we lug a lengthy firearm all that way, enduring a certain amount of difficulty, knowing we will likely only need it for one or two shots, is an irony wasted on the die-hard turkey hunter. You hunt for reasons other than just the killing.

When you tell a non-hunter you traveled all that way for a bird, it can seem a little strange to the listener. The inevitable reference to finding a more affordable option in the frozen food section of your local grocery store gets a little old. No matter. That's their frame of reference.

After your firearm has been inspected and legally checked in, you hoist your baggage up onto the scale. If it tilts to more than 50 pounds you'll be paying an extra fee; less than 50 pounds and you risk not having something you need 1,000 miles away.

Inside that big duffel bag the average turkey hunter has stuffed a lucky hat (and several more should weather turn sour), multiple long-sleeve

TEN HUNTING TRIP MISTAKES

Always trust your guide.

Below: *Your best friend on turkey trips is the camp cook, especially if he's also the guy who makes the pre-dawn coffee.*

1. Failure to read detailed game laws. If you fly to hunt, do study this material above the clouds at 35,000 feet. You can also do so at turkey camp. Print regulations from that state's online website before you travel, or simply contact them for a printed copy.
2. Forgetting to get specific directions to the camp or location you're hunting.
3. Leaving your address book with trip contact telephone numbers at home, or forgetting to punch these into your cell phone.
4. Packing light when you should have done the opposite, or lugging too much on the trip.
5. Not taking a camera along to record those memories. Forgetting batteries for that digital or 35mm camera, or the right film for the latter.

Right: *Prickly pear cactus, and other wild things that stick, poke, or even bite you, mandates that you bring sturdy boots to places like Texas in fall and winter.*

6. Failure to bring a cooler along for your turkey meat—soft for air travel, if it will go inside your luggage; hard for road trips to ride in the back of the truck.
7. Bringing new boots on a trip that will require a lot of breaking in.
8. Forgetting to check updated airline baggage regulations, and travel itineraries for particular carriers.
9. No photo I.D. No driver's license. No passport. No identity.
10. Failure to leave contact details for your family.

I recently turkey hunted Wyoming, and when I called home on arrival, my wife thought I was in Texas and my daughter asked what the weather was like in Kentucky. Bottom line: communicate your whereabouts. Provide lodge phone numbers, names, and your itinerary if possible.

You and your turkey dog have traveled far and done well—enjoy it.

Top: *Some lodges function as unacknowledged turkey hunting museums, with box call collections and other memorabilia offering interesting diversions during downtime.*

camouflage T-shirts, a camo jacket or two, a turkey vest, seat cushion, boots, multiple pairs of leaf-patterned pants, underwear of some sort in triplicate, ammunition in its original box, miscellaneous other items, and many, many socks. You can't lock the checked bag these days. You have to trust all the people who touch that duffel between your point of departure and destination.

Snake boots—necessary in places like Florida swamps and the Texas hills—add enough weight to cause immediate worry as the 50-pound limit goes. Then there's a mesh facemask, gloves, and other sundry items, which can be stuffed inside the vest. Not to mention those turkey calls; you can never have enough, and they have to go somewhere, often in your carry-on bag unless you stash a couple friction calls safely in the locked gun case, room providing.

Now it gets interesting. Personal cameras seem to get more attention during airport security inspections these days, and turkey calls—fragile and unique (well, okay, odd)—definitely raise eyebrows.

"What's this, sir?" I'll get asked. "A turkey call," I'll reply. "For calling turkeys?" they'll query. "Yes," I'll answer. It's all quite puzzling, I'm sure, to the onlooker unfamiliar with our subculture of air-activated, hand-operated, and even folksy wing bone calls made from the bones of a turkey's wing. Silence, heavy and still. "Bones?" The discussion that follows depends on where you travel to and from.

A northern New England airline clerk once remarked that she thought my camouflage-covered shotgun was "pretty" and a security guy in Alabama a couple of years back (a fellow turkey hunter, it turns out) initiated such a long and spirited conversation regarding my box call that his supervisor had to shoot him that look authority figures know so well. In some rural places, airport officials will even ask you point blank: "Get your turkey?" That's heartening. I love that about our kind: we're an extended family of sorts.

After a hunt of several days to a week or so, you rise early in camp and actually shave your mug, ready to come home. At the airport, you've got your bright, cheery, somewhat-sleepy face on. After checking your firearm in, you lift that big bag onto the scales. "Sir, that's a little over 50 pounds, I'm sorry."

What? You look. She's right. You just know she wants to make that joke about women not being the only gender that packs too heavily for trips, but she's too much of a pro to say so. Then it hits you: yesterday you hunted in the rain, hoping to fill your remaining turkey tag. Your dirty clothes are soaked with a pound of water. You've got no choice. Zip goes the zipper, and you don that wet jacket, and pull out a damp T-shirt, and roll that into your carry-on knapsack too. Smile. Apologetic look from the clerk. Hey, it ain't that bad. "Forty-nine pounds, 6 ounces," she grins. You're in.

At any rate, shotgun and baggage checked—and likely your frozen turkey—you safely board the plane trying not to arouse any added suspicion with your strangely shaped devices that make the yelps and clucks of wild turkeys.

You stuff that wet clothing into the overhead compartment, hoping the businessman next to you doesn't fret that your rain-wet heap of camouflage sits next to his expensive folded overcoat. Ignore his hairy eyebrow, arched like a villain's. Press on. Smile. Smile again. You reach into your knapsack, pull out a prized box call, adjust the rubber band that keeps it from rattling, and slide it back in a zippered pocket, then under the seat in front of you.

The businessman in the other aisle seat leans toward you. "Get your turkey?" he queries with a conspiratorial whisper.

On road trips, always bring plenty of water for your turkey dog. It's as essential as your shotgun and shells.

CHAPTER 18

As young hunters begin to demonstrate abilities in the field, let them take on more responsibility during the hunt.

Youth to Future

Up before dawn to hunt local turkeys, I put in several hours waiting on silent birds as the wind gusted and a storm came on, and then motored home to get some work done in this office. I arrived in full head-to-toe camouflage just as my wife Elizabeth prepared to drive our eight-year-old daughter Cora to school. Smiling, I looked in the backseat and said, "Hi, sweet pea." She wrinkled her face up, visibly puzzled, and said: "Daddy, where did you sleep last night?"

Kids come to understand our turkey hunting step by step. Here are a dozen ways to encourage youngsters to hunt:

1. **Keep It Simple:** Remember when you first hunted? Chances are you learned one detail at a time. Don't rush the process. Encourage fun and safety.

2. **It's All Good:** Don't just focus on the kill. Talk about the outdoors in a way that a young hunter can appreciate the natural world around them. Discuss scouting for turkey sign. Talk about food sources. Represent your understanding of the natural world as well by noting songbirds, insect life, and wildflowers. Help them see the big picture.

3. **Avoid Competition:** Sure, later on as the hunter develops toward adulthood, gentle ribbing or boasting at camp is harmless. Still, you want to be sure that you encourage the overall hunt, not the pursuit of ego-driven trophy statistics. Fall and winter hunting is great for this, as every tagged either-sex bird—both juvenile turkeys and adults—can be considered a success.

4. **Praise the Little Things:** Did your son or daughter have a wild turkey answer their yelping? Let them know how proud you are of

221

Remember when you first hunted? Chances are you learned one detail at a time. Don't rush the process. Encourage fun and safety.

them. Did they help find tracks and other sign that led you to a flock? Let them know how important that is. Little things matter.

5. **Don't Skimp on Gear:** Your developing hunter should have the same gear you do so that they can use it, enjoy it, and learn from the mistakes they make with it. Provide them with their own calls. Friction calls are great for starters. They can move to diaphragm calls later. If you're so inclined, encourage them to craft turkey calls with you to appreciate the tradition even more.

6. **Shoot, Shoot, and Shoot:** All hunters, young and old, need to acquire a comfort level of shooting so that when a turkey steps up in range, the shot comes naturally. Gun fit is essential, and many manufacturers offer youth models to facilitate development. Shooting well can only be acquired with regular practice—especially as youth hunters go. Have them pattern loads on turkey targets—or soda pop cans (roughly the size of a turkey head)—to acquire this skill.

7. **Find Some Action:** Small game hunting for squirrels, rabbits, and other available game can provide a way for your young hunter to

In fall and winter turkey hunting, every tagged either-sex bird—both juvenile turkeys and adults—can be considered a success.

use those skills you're teaching. For instance, the skill of sitting still at the base of a broad-trunked tree while waiting for bushytails to appear, then raising your gun slowly as they pass behind a tree, is analogous to turkey hunting.

8. **Let Go a Little:** As young hunters begin to demonstrate abilities in the field, let them take on more responsibility during the hunt. Have them scout a particular location while you do so nearby. After this effort, ask them what they found. Let them feel that pride you do when piecing the puzzle together.

9. **The Sporting Tradition:** Instill a notion of hunter ethics and sportsmanship in your son or daughter. Take them to turkey camp with you. Let them experience the hunt. Let them call in a turkey for you. Let it happen under your watchful, positive guidance.

10. **Location, Location, Location:** Seek out a spot on a property you lease alone, where it's just you and your daughter turkey hunting. Take your son on a booked trip someplace special. Public lands can be competitive at times, and that challenge will come soon enough. So for now, try to control the conditions to make it more enjoyable and relaxed.

Cooperate with state agencies and register your fall or winter wild turkey by computer-automated service, or by taking that tagged bird to a checking station. New York State requests that hunters save a leg from a bird—an age indicator—so that biologists might study it.

11. **Safety Issues:** Explain safety issues surely and simply. Don't lecture, scold, or yell. Try to picture yourself as a young hunter. What kind of instruction helped you? Try to model that positive approach.

12. **Make Them Your Hunting Buddy:** Too many sportsmen are caught up in posting big trophy numbers for personal bragging rights, leaving the pure enjoyment behind. Sure, outfoxing and finally tagging a longbeard with sharp spurs and hefty weight is fine on a personal level, but it's also equal to having a young hunter take a fall hen with you on an October hunt. Don't leave them behind. Take them along.

MAKING IT HAPPEN

Cody Evans, age 12, and his dad slowly moved ahead of me in the dark field, as Kevin alternately beamed his flashlight to the ground before snapping it off just as fast. A flock of wild turkeys slept on tree limbs nearby, waiting for early light to seep into the eastern sky.

Turkey registration at checking stations helps wildlife managers plan fall, winter, and spring seasons.

The early autumn chill felt good after September's lingering blasts of heat, a time when I'd bowhunted New Hampshire turkeys. Now I'd motored six hours from my home to hunt New York State on their fall turkey season's opening weekend. Kevin and I had enjoyed autumn hunts before; this was the first time I'd done it with his growing son, now legal hunting age.

We sat down at the base of two broad tree trunks, Cody and Kevin a few steps away off my right shoulder. Autumn shooting hours for turkeys don't arrive until sunrise in New York, so we waited in the dark for the woods to wake up. The roost wasn't far away, and we'd slinked in there undetected. As the false dawn approached a half-hour before the real one, we heard soft tree calling coming from a nearby roost. Turkeys were waking up.

Flapping wings through leaves and branches said one bird had just flown down. Slowly I checked my watch face: fifteen minutes until sunrise. Other turkey talk commenced. The flock's brood hen assembly yelped down the hill, not far from the field we'd walked through in the dark. Cody's dad and I had softly called since that first bird started. We'd have to keep these turkeys interested until official shooting hours arrived.

One bird slowly moved through the multiflora rose in front of their father-son setup. As Kevin softly clucked, the turkey looked, waited, and softly answered. This particular bird froze decoy-like for much of the time, and only now and again could I see its head and neck looking for the source of the calling. The intensity that comes from waiting like this, knowing you might be detected at any second, is also why we hunt. It's a sweet agony that promises a possible payoff.

Soon, another turkey crashed down from a tree branch, calling as soon as it hit the ground. As is typical of young fall hens and gobblers, they'll often group together first before moving toward the brood hen in small numbers. That was happening right in front of us.

Moving only my eyes, I could see the two camouflaged tree stumps that were Cody and Kevin waiting, holding steady. Young Evans had been in on this deal before. Just that past spring he'd taken his first turkey with his dad along, a fine spring gobbler. Now he was after his first autumn bird. He'd soon get his chance.

My watch, its face on the inside of my wrist so that I could read it while my left hand gripped the shotgun's forend, now said legal time had arrived. Great, the birds were still here, as the hen yelped her commands.

Through the ground cover, I saw one, two, then three birds together. Both Kevin and I issued kee-kees, and kee-kee-runs, the calls of autumn's juvenile birds-of-the-year. Real turkeys answered back. As we called, several turkeys moved out of the thicker cover, around to my side of things. Now in view, two turkeys walked in together. We had to wait for them to step apart.

I peeled an eye toward Cody, saw that the birds were a bit too far to his left, and resolved to make a shot if it came. It did. A turkey stood tall, called, and at that I pulled the trigger. Cody's shot followed as a bird flew-hopped from where it stood next to mine, and landed in range and sight of young Evans.

Veteran turkey hunters might have wilted under the pressure, but not Cody. He kept his composure and dropped a bird with one shotgun report. Game over. We'd doubled. Such moments are special for those of us who've hunted for decades, and it was a privilege to share it with this father and son.

LEAD BY EXAMPLE

There's more to a wild turkey hunt than the killing. It's the camaraderie at camp, discussing past hunts, and plans for future outings. It's listening

Veteran hunters might have wilted under the pressure, but not Cody Evans. He kept his composure and dropped his first autumn turkey with one shotgun report. Game over. We'd doubled.

You may have shot that turkey, but someone else—be it the landowner, your hardworking guide, or the management effort that helped sustain the bird in that habitat—always figures into the wild turkey you've tagged.

for birds clawing up to their roost trees, and being there when they fly down in the morning. It's putting together the patchwork of turkey sign, and arriving at an understanding of how a particular turkey flock moves through its range. It's enjoying the vocabulary of the wild turkey, and attempting to master those calls yourself. It's being aware of the tradition's history. It's taking a turkey by fair chase, employing acceptable sporting techniques, and abiding by game laws. It's reliving that hunt at the supper table.

We should try to convey this unique pursuit to young hunters by emphasizing the hunt over the kill. Trophy standards of measuring spurs, checking beard length, and assessing weight are fine. I've done it myself, and taken pride in the accomplishment. These numerical details can help us age a particular turkey and provide a certain fascination as that goes. However, when such trophy standards fuel only the turkey hunter's competitive ego, there's something missing. And in the end, hunts always involve a "we" over an "I" effort.

You may have shot that turkey, but someone else—be it the land-owner, your hardworking guide, or the management effort that helped sustain the bird in that habitat—always figures into the wild turkey you've tagged. Remember that, and pass your love of the hunt on.

THE FUTURE OF FALL AND WINTER TURKEY HUNTING

Certainly, the next generation of hunters will serve to further the tradition. These days, let's face it, quality spring turkey hunting receives much of the emphasis and attention, in part since permits and sportsman effort are extended beyond the traditional autumn and winter seasons. This, in short, generates additional money for state wildlife agencies. There's also an entire generation of hunters who target beards in the spring and antlers in the fall. That's fine of course, so long as the autumn and winter tradition is understood, respected, and represented.

As alluded to in the previous chapter, management responses in relation to fall turkey hunting are varied across our nation. Some states create management zones based on habitat, which directly affects huntable flock populations. Turkeys in large forested areas see less pressure than those in compromised, fragmented habitats. Agencies react accordingly.

Another way is to limit fall and winter seasons, based primarily on time and length. At times wildlife managers do so to stage fall turkey seasons before or after deer opportunities. Opportunities can also be structured to include specific license quotas, which limit hunter numbers, and bag limits, which control tagged birds.

Since accurate population numbers are at best guesswork, it's important that turkey hunters cooperate with agencies that ask successful sportsmen to register their fall or winter hen or gobbler by computer-automated service or by taking that wild turkey to a checking station. New York State goes one step further and requests that hunters save a leg from a bird they've taken so that biologists might observe it. You should be happy to comply with these efforts as an indication of your seriousness as a hunter, but still, some officials routinely indicate more participation is necessary.

FULL CIRCLE

This spring, I noted a large defecated once-a-day stool on a grassy trail rimming a green pasture along wooded edge cover indicating a nearby hen was sitting nearly 24/7. As always, I made a note to check back there at a later date in hopes of finding her brood moving behind her, indicating the hatch for this particular turkey had been successful. Sure enough, weeks later, on a steamy June morning, I found her standing tall not far from where I sensed she'd been nesting, with eight poults bobbing along behind—the circle completed.

Though challenges lurk for this brood and others, all in all, the future for spring, fall, and winter turkey hunting seems bright, so long as gobblers and hens breed, poults hatch, and there are enough of us around who care about this ongoing cycle.

Wild turkeys, and our meaningful hunting tradition, matter. If you've hung in there until the end of this book, I'm sure you agree.

Though challenges lurk for this flock and others, all in all, the future for spring, fall, and winter turkey hunting seems bright, so long as gobblers and hens breed, poults hatch, and there are enough of us around who care about this ongoing cycle.

APPENDIX

RECOMMENDED READING

Most modern wild turkey books emphasize the spring hunt over a fall/winter focus, which is why you have this title in your hands right now. I've read and enjoyed many.

On downtime, you can read such titles—including the abbreviated list I share here—for vicarious pleasure, learning about particular strategies, experiences, and even technical information shared by specific writers. Even seemingly unrelated material might help shape your sense of fall and winter turkey hunting. As history, practical know-how, and even cooking wild turkeys goes, here are some places to look:

Bland, Dwain. *Turkey Hunter's Digest.* Northbrook, IL: DBI Books, Inc., 1986. Bland reflects an enthusiasm for wild turkeys that involves fall, winter, and spring hunting.

Casada, Jim. *America's Greatest Game Bird: Archibald Rutledge's Turkey-Hunting Tales.* Columbia, SC: University of South Carolina Press, 1994. Edited and selected by Dr. Casada, this satisfying collection captures a bygone time period and represents Rutledge's turkey writing, including autumn and winter stories. If you want to know what it was like to turkey hunt in the first half of the twentieth century, get your hands on this compilation.

Davis, Henry E. *The American Wild Turkey.* Georgetown, SC: Small-Arms Technical Publishing Company, 1949. An exact photographic reproduction of this vital work was reprinted in 1984 by Old Masters Publishers of Medon, Tennessee. Davis's work is a heavy dose of how-to writing and is full of strategies that are still applicable today, while others seem antiquated in these modern times.

Dickson, James G. *The Wild Turkey: Biology & Management.* Mechanicsburg, PA: Stackpole Books, 1992. Edited by Dickson, there's no better collected text on wild turkey background, history, biology, habitat, and management through the early 1990s. Much of this scientific data is useful to the well-schooled turkey hunter.

Henderson, David R. *The Ultimate Guide to Shotgunning.* Guilford, CT: The Lyons Press, 2003. This comprehensive guide on shotguns also provides a chapter on turkey hunting.

Hutto, Joe. *Illumination in the Flatwoods.* New York: The Lyons Press, 1995. No book better reflects an understanding of the wild turkey's flock behavior from egg toward adulthood than this one. Here, naturalist Hutto establishes his human imprint on egg-incubated turkey poults, then records their relationship in journal-entry style.

Irmscher, Christoph. *John James Audubon: Writings & Drawings.* New York, NY: The Library of America, 1999. Selected by Irmscher, Audubon's wild turkey writing presented here provides a historical glimpse into the nineteenth century world of the wild turkey, including hunting strategies prevalent at the time.

Livingston, A. D. *Wild Turkey Cookbook.* Mechanicsburg, PA: Stackpole Books, 1995. This useful collection of recipes offers plenty of ways to extend your hunt to the kitchen.

McIlhenny, Edward A. *The Wild Turkey and Its Hunting.* Garden City, NY: Doubleday, Page & Company, 1914. As with the Davis book, Old Masters Publishers reprinted this title in 1984 as well. While McIlhenny's name is installed as the author, Charles L. Jordan (shot by a poacher in 1909) is responsible for much of the writing and all of the photographs included in this book. The chapter on dogging turkeys is a must-read for modern canine enthusiasts.

Turkey Call. Various issues. Early 1970s-present. *TC* is the National Wild Turkey Federation's print magazine (six issues annually). Inclusive Sept./Oct. and Nov./Dec. offerings from 2000 to the present have placed a particular emphasis on autumn and winter hunting as wild turkey populations continue to grow nationwide and opportunities increase.

Turkey & Turkey Hunting. Various issues. Early 1990s-present. The fall issue of *T&TH* focuses on the autumn tradition, while other material serves to inform and entertain the year-round turkey hunter. Biologist Lovett E. Williams, Jr., and Editor-at-Large Jim Casada, among others, routinely contribute to this publication.

Williams, Ben O. *Bird Dog: The Instinctive Training Method.* Minocqua, WI: Willow Creek Press, 2002. While the book contains nothing on fall and winter turkey hunting, I honestly believe this is one of the best titles on training bird dogs (and I've read many). Applying Williams's information in the field will help both neophyte and veteran turkey doggers build an essential bond with their canine hunting partners.

Williams, Lovett E. *Wild Turkey Country.* Gary Griffen, contributing photographer. Minocqua, WI: Willow Creek Press, 1991. Griffen's superb color images along with biologist Williams's accompanying text make this an instructive and enjoyable coffee table book that illustrates the year-round life of the wild turkey.

You should also read, reread, and carry with you state hunting regulations wherever you chase fall and winter wild turkeys. A routine online search for specific wildlife agencies will yield websites that provide more up-to-date information to help you plan your fall and winter turkey hunts.

GEAR TO GO

You have your favorites, and I have mine. What follows is a list of manufacturers whose products have figured prominently in my turkey hunts.

Camouflage, because you have to hide:

Jordan Outdoor Enterprises, Ltd.
1390 Box Circle
Columbus, Georgia 31907
800-992-9968
www.realtree.com
Realtree/Advantage camouflage
patterns.

Mossy Oak
3330 Cumberland Blvd.
Atlanta, Georgia 30339-5985
800-331-5624
www.mossyoak.com
Mossy Oak apparel and other
products.

Natural Gear
5310 S. Shackleford Rd., Suite D
Little Rock, Arkansas 72204
800-628-4327
www.naturalgear.com
Natural Gear camouflage patterns.

Skyline Camouflage
3984 Burke Parkway, Suite 2
Blasdell, New York 14219
877-650-7591
www.skylinecamo.com
Skyline camouflage patterns.

*Ammunition, because without it, it's
catch-and-release hunting:*

Federal Premium Ammunition
Federal Cartridge Co.
900 Ehlen Drive
Anoka, Minnesota 55303
800-322-2342
www.federalcartridge.com

Hevi-Shot/Environ-Metal, Inc.
P.O. Box 834
1307 Clark Mill Rd.
Sweet Home, Oregon 97386
541-367-3522
www.hevishot.com

Remington Arms Company, Inc.
870 Remington Drive
Madison, North Carolina 27025
800-243-9700
www.remington.com

Winchester Ammunition
427 North Shamrock
East Alton, Illinois 62024
www.winchester.com

*Shotguns, because you need to put that
ammo somewhere:*

Browning/U.S. Repeating Arms
One Browning Place
Morgan, Utah 84050
800-234-2069
www.browning.com

Remington Arms Company, Inc.
870 Remington Drive
Madison, North Carolina 27025
800-243-9700
www.remington.com

Calls, because you need to talk turkey:

Hunter's Specialties
6000 Huntington Ct. NE
Cedar Rapids, Iowa 52402
319-395-0321
www.hunterspec.com

Quaker Boy Game Calls
5455 Webster Road
Orchard Park, New York 14127
800-544-1600
www.quakerboygamecalls.com

Woods Wise Products
P.O. Box 681552
Franklin, Tennessee 37068
800-735-8182
www.woodswise.com

Boots, because of mud, rocks, prickly pear cactus, creeks, swamps, and snakes:

Lacrosse Footwear, Inc.
18550 NE Riverside Parkway
Portland, Oregon 97230
800-323-2668
www.lacrosse-outdoors.com

The Original Muck Boot Company
1136 Second St.
Rock Island, Illinois 61201
877-GET-MUCK
www.muckbootcompany.com

Rocky Brands
39 E. Canal St.
Nelsonville, Ohio 45764
740-753-1951
www.rockyboots.com

Mail-order catalog companies which offer turkey-chasing gear, because you'd rather hunt than shop:

Bass Pro Shops
2500 E. Kearney
Springfield, Missouri 65898-0123
800-227-7776
www.basspro.com

Cabela's
One Cabela Drive
Sidney, Nebraska 69160
800-237-4444
www.cabelas.com

L.L.Bean
Freeport, Maine 04033
800-221-4221
www.llbean.com

Miscellaneous manufacturers, because they offer some other products you might need:

Atsko/Sno-Seal, Inc.
2664 Russell S.E.
Orangeburg, SC 29115
800-845-2728
www.atsko.com
Products to keep your feet dry on stormy fall and winter hunts.

DeLorme Mapping Company
Two DeLorme Dr.
Yarmouth, Maine 04096
800-561-5105
www.delorme.com
I mark my DeLorme *Atlas and Gazetteers* with a handwritten "T" where I find turkeys while scouting or hunting.

Streamlight
30 Eagleville Road
Eagleville, Pennsylvania 19403
800-523-7488
www.streamlight.com
Consider their thin, pocket-friendly penlights an essential item for the pre-dawn and post-dusk hours as you enter and exit the woods.

UnderArmour
1020 Hull St.
Baltimore, Maryland 21230
888-4-ARMOUR
www.underarmour.com
Their superb undergarments will
make you turn your old-school long
johns into gun-cleaning rags. Strongly
recommended for autumn and winter
turkey hunts.

A place that offers turkey dog hunts,
because you may want to try it:

Turkey Trot Acres
Pete and Sherry Clare
188 Tubbs Hill Road
Candor, New York 13743
607-659-7849
turkeytrot@frontiernet.net
www.turkeytrotacres.com
This is the best operation for fall
turkey hunting in the country. Their
Appalachian turkey dog hunts on
autumn flocks are unrivaled, and
done with great respect to the tradition. Food and lodging are first-rate as
well.

And finally, the NWTF, because they
share your love of this hunting tradition:

National Wild Turkey Federation
The Wild Turkey Center
770 Augusta Road
Edgefield, South Carolina 29824-1510
800-THE-NWTF
www.nwtf.org

INDEX